GLOW-IN-THE-DARK FISH

B. J. REINHARD

Glow-in-the-Dark Fish and 59 More Ways to See God Through His Creation
Copyright © 2000
B.J. Reinhard

Design by Lookout Design Group, Inc.
Cover and text illustrations by Greg Cross

Published by Bethany House Publishers
A Ministry of Bethany Fellowship, Inc.
11400 Hampshire Avenue South
Minneapolis, Minnesota 55438
www.bethanyhouse.com

Printed in the United States of America

Library of Congress Cataloging-in-Publication Data
Reinhard, B.J.
    Glow-in-the-dark fish and 59 more ways to see God through his creation / by Barbara Reinhard.
        p. cm.
Summary: Sixty short devotional readings introduce the biological sciences as indications of God's creativity and are accompanied by relevant scripture verses and suggested activities.
    ISBN 0–7642–2262–7
    1. Creation—Juvenile literature. 2. Biology—Religious aspects—Christianity—Juvenile literature. 3. Children—Prayer-books and devotions—English. [1. Biology—Religious aspects. 2. Prayer books and devotions.] I. Title.
    BT695.5 .R442 2000
    242'.62—dc21   00-008272

For Steve and my Lord
You made me dance

About the Author

B. J. Reinhard's love for writing and nature began when she was a teenager in Colorado. She still lives in Colorado, where she enjoys the company of her husband, their two sons, a spunky yellow lab, multitudinous African violets, and a pet carniverous plant.

TABLE of Contents

INTRODUCTION

Have you ever passed by something time after time

and never quite noticed it? Then one day you pass by it again, and suddenly you see it—really see it—for the first time?

I was on a walk one spring evening, years ago, when that happened to me.

The day was no different from any other. Accompanied by my giant white dog, I traveled the same route that I always traveled: across a field, over to a middle school, and along a grassy area planted with a row of young evergreens not much taller than I was.

For some reason, I stopped—I don't remember why. But what I do remember is that the new growth on the first tree caught my attention. These needles were a gentle lime green, lighter in color than the rest of the tree. They were feathery, flexible, and soft to the touch. Some, still bundled in brown, papery sheaths opened just slightly when I set them free. I remember my delight as I pulled off one sheath after another.

And then I had The Thought. It was a thought so different from my usual way of thinking that it startled me. *If there's a God who made this tree, then He's a God I could know.*

Several years passed before I would discover that it *was* God who made that tree, and that He *is* a God I can know. During those years, my curiosity about nature grew. And today my delight and wonder in His creation is much greater than it was when He first revealed himself to me. Maybe that's because even the ordinary things of this world take on beauty when you know that God made them. And then when you consider glow-in-the-dark fish—WOW!

This book about our living world was written with the hope that you, too, will discover God through His creation. An even greater hope is that in discovering Him, you will seek to know Him more deeply.

Each reading describes something from the world of science that relates to a theme about God and your life. A Bible verse and **Thought to remember** are included to encourage you.

The Bible verses listed are meant to encourage you, too. At first it may seem easiest to just skip over them. But you might be surprised by what God shows you if you ask Him to reveal himself to you through them!

Words that might stretch your **vocabulary** are in bold type. You can learn what they mean and how to say them if you take a step over to the margin—just like it's shown here.

vocabulary:
(vo-CAB-you-
Lare-ee)
the group of
words you
know and use

For hands-on fun that builds on the topic featured in each reading, check out the activities. Be sure to check with your parents before trying them! Answers to the puzzle activities are at the back of the book, starting on page 151.

If you'd like to explore more about any topic, **Dig Deeper!** lists key words and phrases you can use in a library or Internet search.

As you turn the page to begin *Glow-in-the-Dark Fish*, think of yourself as beginning an adventure—an adventure to discover more about our world and our God.

The Master Plan

P icture a starfish. What does it have in common with a snowflake and a daisy?

Picture a snail shell. How is it similar to the curled horn of a mountain sheep and an ordinary spider web? Now picture a tree. What does it have in common with an antler and a dragonfly wing?

Perhaps you noticed that the objects in each of these groups share a similar design. The shapes of starfish, snowflakes, and daisies are based on a star. Each has arms—or rays—that grow out of a center.

Snail shells, mountain sheep horns, and the sticky threads of ordinary spider webs are based on a **spiral** design. This design starts at the heart and coils around and around and around and around.

Trees, antlers, and the veins on dragonfly wings are branch shaped. In each of these, arms fan out from a main shaft.

Once you start looking around, you'll notice patterns everywhere in nature. Circles are found on leopard fur, peacock feathers, and in the eyes of owls. You'll notice six-sided **hexagons** that make up bee honeycombs, the bumps on turtle shells, and the eyes of flies.

Some designs are hidden. Inside whale flippers, human arms, frog legs, and bat and bird wings are bones that are put together with the same pattern.

Some patterns take a sharp eye. That's the case with **Fibonacci** numbers. These numbers are formed by adding the two numbers before it. For example, if you add one plus one, you get two. Then if you add one plus two, you get three. Two plus three equals five. Three plus five is eight. If you write all these numbers down, you get a string of numbers that looks like this: 1, 1, 2, 3, 5, 8, 13, 21, 34, 55, 89, 144, 233 . . .

What's so special about Fibonacci numbers? They're found all over nature. If you look at the seed head of a sunflower, your eye recognizes spirals. Counting them, you find that thirty-four spin counterclockwise. Fifty-five spirals spin clockwise. On giant sunflowers fifty-five spirals go one direction, eighty-nine the other. Check the line of

spiral:
(SPY-rul)

hexagon:
(HEK-suh-gone)

Fibonacci:
(Fee-buh-NAH-chee) an Italian mathematician who discovered number patterns in nature. He lived from 1170–1250 A.D. His real name was Leonardo da Pisa.

> "You are worthy, our Lord and God! You are worthy to receive glory and honor and power. You are worthy because you created all things. They were created and they exist. That is the way you planned it."
>
> REVELATION 4:11

What's special about the hexagon shape of honeycombs? Each side fits against the side of another hexagon. The wall of one cell doubles as the wall of another. There are no empty spaces between them, so bees save on building materials.

DISCOVER IT!

Buy a pineapple or find a pinecone. Use a marker to paint a dot on the scales going clockwise. Use a different color to mark the scales going counterclockwise. Use a third color to mark the scales going straight up. Count the number of spirals going each direction. Are they Fibonacci numbers?

EXPLORE IT!

Figure out the next three Fibonacci numbers to follow those listed on page 11.

The answers are on page 151.

DIG DEEPER!

★ patterns in nature
★ design in nature
★ Fibonacci numbers

Fibonacci numbers above. These numbers are next to each other on the Fibonacci scale!

Pinecones and pineapples also share the fun of Fibonacci. Counting spirals from the stem end of some pinecones reveals five gradual spirals rising from the left to the right. Eight steep spirals rise from the right to the left. Other cones show different Fibonacci combinations: three and five, eight and thirteen.

The outside of a pineapple is covered with hexagon-shaped bumps, or scales. Each pineapple has spirals that rotate in three directions: one spiral that twists to the right, one that twists to the left, and one that rises nearly straight up. The number of scales in each of these spirals? Eight, thirteen, and twenty-one. Are these numbers next to each other on the Fibonacci scale? Yes!

Some scientists would like us to believe that the patterns appearing in nature happen by chance.

What do you think? Can patterns that repeat themselves such as these just happen by chance or accident?

It's not likely. Patterns show there's a master plan for nature. It's the Master's plan. God is the Designer.

Perhaps some people have a hard time believing that God created the earth because He's invisible to our eyes. Yet what He created is not invisible. There's no escaping it—God's fingerprints are on everything He made. We're surrounded by stars, spirals, branches, circles, and hexagons. We're surrounded by Fibonacci numbers. Through the awesome designs in our world, we see God. We understand His greatness.

Because God is so detailed in His designs, it's not a stretch to believe that He can easily care about the details of our lives, too. Does He care that you're feeling lonely? Does He care that your mom got mad at you this morning? Does He care that you're having a hard time at school? Yes, He does!

The same God who so carefully designed nature also designed you. He designed the details of your life. Through them He shows His care for you.

Thought to remember:

God cares about the details of nature. He cares about the details of my life.

Additional verses:

Romans 1:20; Psalm 19:1–4; Genesis 1:1; Psalm 139:1–4, 13–16

Voice of a Flower

There's a constant battle for our attention in this world. TV commercials lure us with fast clips of beautiful people, bright colors, and catchy tunes. Radio messages charm us with snappy sayings and songs. Magazine ads grab our attention with flashy pictures and, sometimes, smells. All promise to give us something we desire. By appealing to our senses of sight and sound, advertisements make us want to buy.

In nature, plants also advertise themselves to the world. The colors, smells, and shapes of flowers draw bats, birds, butterflies, and other beasts near. They promise to give these creatures something they want—nectar or pollen for food.

Why do plants advertise themselves? Plants need these creatures to help them produce seeds.

In the middle of flowers are male and female parts. The male part of a plant produces tiny grains called **pollen**. Pollen from the male part must reach the female part in order for seeds to develop. This is called **pollination**. Some flowers need help getting pollen from the male to the female part. That's where animals come in. When an animal visits a flower, pollen sticks to feathers or fur. When that animal visits another flower of the same kind, pollen brushes off onto the female parts to pollinate the flower.

Many flowers that open during the day use bright colors to lure pollinators. Bees are drawn to blue and yellow flowers, especially if they're sweet-smelling. Many butterflies prefer blue, violet, and yellow flowers, although some are attracted to red. Birds have a weak sense of smell; odorless pink and red flowers are often pollinated by birds. Bats and moths visit pale or white flowers. Why? At nighttime, darkness dulls colors, but white flowers reflect moonlight and starlight. These flowers also depend on heavy, sweet perfumes to reel in pollinators.

Shapes are also tailored to specific critters. Only creatures with extra long beaks or tongues can reach all the way into long, trumpet-shaped flowers. Birds and bats need flowers with sturdy petals to perch on while they sip nectar.

POLLEN:
(PAZZ-en)

POLLINATION:
(PALL-ih-NA-SHUN)

To discover more about what happens during pollination, turn to "Fruit Facts" on page 134.

> EVER SINCE THE WORLD WAS CREATED IT HAS BEEN POSSIBLE TO SEE THE QUALITIES OF GOD THAT ARE NOT SEEN. I'M TALKING ABOUT HIS ETERNAL POWER AND ABOUT THE FACT THAT HE IS GOD. THOSE THINGS CAN BE SEEN IN WHAT HE HAS MADE.
>
> ROMANS 1:20

More flower facts:

* One type of orchid copies the smell, color, shape, and size of a certain female wasp. The confused male wasp that tries to mate with the orchid is dusted with pollen.
* Flowers don't always lure pollinators with odors we like. Several flowers smell like rotting meat. Some are even dark red like meat. These stinky blossoms attract flies.
* The hawkmoth is the only animal with a tongue long enough to reach all the way inside the fourteen-inch throat of a certain flower from the orchid family.
* Flowers often give clues to guide pollinators to nectar. These lines, spots, and colors point to the center where nectar can be found.

DRAW IT!

This activity is to help you to look carefully. Draw a picture of a living flower, then color it in. The design of a flower is awesome, isn't it? What about its color and shape? What type of creatures might your flower invite near?

DIG DEEPER!

* pollination
* flowers
* plants
* insects and flowers

Some **orchids** go to a lot of trouble to spread their pollen. The bucket orchid is one of them. A certain type of bee visits this flower to collect a special oil. Slipping off a waxy knob of the orchid, the bee tumbles into a pool of liquid. As it thrashes about, the bee finds a step that leads to a tunnel. At the end of the tunnel, the bee is locked in a tight trap, where a pollen packet is stuck to its back. Then the trap relaxes and the bee is freed. It flies off to visit another bucket orchid, which receives this gift of pollen.

The colors, fragrances, and shapes of flowers get the attention of bats, birds, butterflies, and other beasts. They grab ours, too. Perhaps you've stood in amazement at the sight of a field purple with wild flowers. Or perhaps you've caught the scent of a bouquet of roses and buried your face right in the middle of them to enjoy their heavenly scent.

Like mountains, oceans, stars in the sky . . . flowers are a way for God to get our attention, to get us to draw near. Then through them, He speaks to us. We might hear something like this: "If you're amazed as you look into the face of a pansy, it's because I made it." Then we understand that the One who made the world is even more amazing. Nature is an expression of God. It reflects the Creator and gives us a glimpse of how awesome He is.

But God isn't satisfied with our just knowing that He's the Creator. He wants us to know *Him*. So we might also hear, "You came near to my flowers, now come near to me. I want you to get to know me. Let's be friends."

God reveals a bit of himself through nature. But as we seek to know God, we discover that He reveals himself fully through Jesus. It's through Jesus that God expresses His care for us. It's through Jesus that we grow close to God.

Thought to remember:

God reveals himself to me through creation and through His Son, Jesus.

Additional verses:

Psalm 19:1–4a; 27:4; Genesis 1:11–12; John 1:1–4; 17:3; Colossians 2:9

Many insects see **ultraviolet** (ul-truh-VY-uh-let) light, wavelengths of light invisible to us. Many flowers have ultraviolet markings to attract and guide pollinators.

Orchid: (OR-kid) a family of showy flowers. Many have three petals: one shaped like a lip and two that look like wings. Women often wear these flowers on special days.

3 THE PLAGUE

Step into a time machine for a trip back in time.

The year is 1348. The place, Florence, Italy. As soon as you step from the time machine, you notice that an awful smell fills the air. Bodies of people lie in the streets. Nearby, a person too weak to move, groans. Egg-sized growths swell from the area below his ears. Dark purple blotches stain his skin.

A priest walks by. Behind him a body is carried on a board. Following the priest, you arrive at a church. A large trench in the churchyard is filled with bodies. Only a thin layer of dirt covers them.

You run from the scene, hoping to escape. Just what kind of nightmare is this?

It's the **bubonic plague**, also called Black Death. This disease spread from Italy throughout Europe in the mid-1300s. Caused by a rod-shaped **bacteria**, bubonic plague is carried by fleas. A flea picks up the disease when it bites an infected rat. The bacteria multiplies inside the flea's stomach. Then, when it bites another rat, the bacteria is passed on. Sometimes infected fleas bite humans.

> "She will give birth to a son, and you are to give him the name Jesus, because he will save his people from their sins."
>
> MATTHEW 1:21

In the fourteenth century, rats swarmed garbage-littered streets and invaded houses. Once the rats' fleas became infected with Black Death, the disease spread like fire from rats to humans. During a span of three to four years, about 25,000,000 people are believed to have died from the plague.

The most noticeable sign of bubonic plague is egg-sized swellings in the **groin**, armpits, and neck. High fever, chills, and a headache add to the misery. At least half the people who came down with bubonic plague died. Death came quickly—within three to five days.

Today, bubonic plague is far less common. Rat populations are reduced by careful control of garbage. This lessens the chances for the plague to get started and spread. And if a person does come down with the plague today, we have a weapon to fight it—antibiotics.

Before antibiotics, the plague swept through Europe, affecting the lives of all who lived there. There's another disease that affects every person born into this world. It's

bubonic plague: (boo-BAWN-ik playg)

bacteria: (back-TEER-ee-ah) a very small form of life that can be seen only with the help of a microscope

groin: (rhymes with coin) where the top of your leg and the bottom of your body meet

To discover more about bacteria, turn to "Spoiled Rotten" on page 137.

SPIRIT:
(SPIHR-it) the
part inside you
where God lives

a disease of the **spirit**, called sin.

When Adam disobeyed God in the Garden of Eden, sin entered the world. From then on all humans were born wanting their own way instead of God's. What's the result of sin? Death. Everyone in this world eventually dies. Spiritual death—being separated from God—is also a result of sin.

The people of Europe were helpless to save themselves from bubonic plague. We're also helpless when it comes to sin, the disease of our spirits. But God has given us a cure. The cure is His Son, Jesus. When Jesus died on the cross, He suffered for us. He took all of our sin sickness on himself.

Suppose you came down with the plague. You'd visit a doctor, and he'd give you an antibiotic. Would you take it? Of course you would! It wouldn't help unless you did.

The same is true for sin. God's cure for sin does no good unless we take Jesus as our Savior. How do we do that? By turning to God and believing that Jesus will save us from the disease of our sin. Taking an antibiotic is easy. Believing in Jesus is, too.

Thought to remember:
Jesus heals me of sin.

Additional verses:
Romans 5:12, 18–19; Isaiah 53:4–6; Psalm 103:2–3; Jeremiah 17:14 (NIV); Acts 3:19; 16:31

FIND IT!
In the following sentences, darken the letters by the statements that are false. The letters that remain spell out the cure for sin.

S Plague is spread mostly by fleas on dogs.
J A bacteria causes bubonic plague.
F Plague is spread by mosquitoes.
E Sin affects everyone.
B We can save ourselves from sin.
S Plague can be cured by antibiotics.
U Rats like to live in garbage.
T Another name for plague is Purple Death.
S Fleas can jump from rats to humans.

The answers are on page 151.

DIG DEEPER!
* bubonic plague
* Black Death
* epidemic
* rats and disease
* fleas

4 Got Life?

How can you tell if something is alive?

If something grows, moves, or uses energy, does that mean it's alive? Clouds "grow," but they're definitely not alive. Cars move and use energy, but they're not alive, either. Flames also "grow," and they move and use energy, too. But would you say flames have life?

How *can* you tell if something is alive or not? What is the difference between a cloud and a clam? A car and a cat? Or flames and a fire ant?

Nonliving things may grow, move, or use energy. But they don't share *all* the qualities that are true of living things. Let's take a closer look. . . .

All living things are made up of tiny units called **cells**. These are organized to form larger parts. In your body, you know some of these parts as your heart, stomach, lungs, legs, and arms.

cell: (sell)

In order for these parts to do their job, they need energy. This comes from food. Food is broken down inside your body so you can grow. Your body also needs food to maintain and repair itself.

You need energy to move, too. Like other living things, you can move by yourself. You can run, walk, and do somersaults. When you need food, you pluck an apple from a tree or open the refrigerator door. Of course plants can't do any of these, but they can bend toward the sun, the source of their food.

> Here is God's witness. He has given us eternal life. That life is found in His Son. Those who belong to the Son have life. Those who do not belong to the Son of God do not have life.
>
> 1 JOHN 5:11–12

Living things also respond to their surroundings. The warmth of the sun feels good. But if it's too hot, you head for the shade to cool off. If you see a good friend, you approach him. But a snarling dog has the opposite effect!

reproduce: (ree-pruh-DUCE) to produce children

All living things eventually die. That's why there's another shared quality among things that are alive: They **reproduce.**

Before they die, living things produce children that resemble their parents. You are similar to your parents, who are similar to their parents, who are similar to *their* parents. And like all living things, when you were born you started out much smaller

Have you ever had the flu or common cold? These diseases are caused by **viruses** (VY-russ-ez). Some biologists—scientists who study life—don't think viruses are alive. Why? They don't have cells. They use the cells of other living things for energy and to reproduce.

EXPLORE IT!

Ask your parents for old magazines. Cut out pictures and sort them into groups of living and non-living things. Make a collage out of your pictures by gluing them onto a large sheet of paper or poster board. Put the living things on one half and the nonliving things on the other half.

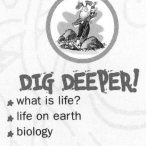

DIG DEEPER!

* what is life?
* life on earth
* biology

than you are now. As you continue to grow, your body develops. When you become an adult, you'll be able to have children of your own. And they will be similar to you.

Your need for food, and your ability to move, to respond to your surroundings, to develop, grow, and reproduce are qualities that you share with every living thing. They show that you have **physical** life.

Did you know you can have **spiritual** life, too? Just as you're born physically, you must also be born spiritually. Your first birth comes from your earthly parents. But how can you be born a second time? Is it by going to church, by being baptized, or by being nice?

Spiritual life comes only from God. Your second birth comes from the Spirit of God when you believe in Jesus. Then you have Jesus' life inside you.

Just as physical life needs energy to function, spiritual life does, too. This energy comes from Jesus' living inside you. His energy is needed for you to grow and develop and respond to God.

Another quality that spiritual life shares with physical life is the ability to reproduce. Through you, others learn about God. If they believe in Jesus, they become God's children, too. All of us who are God's children resemble our heavenly Father, just as each of us resembles our earthly parents.

Even though your physical life eventually will come to an end, your spiritual life will go on forever. The life of God is eternal; His life never ends. You can be sure that even if your body dies, your spirit will continue to live on in heaven with God.

PHYSICAL: (FIH-zih-kul) Having to do with the body

SPIRITUAL: (SPIHR-ih-chew-ul) Having to do with the Spirit

Thought to remember:
Jesus gives me spiritual life.

Additional verses:
John 3:3–7, 16; 10:10b; 14:6

5 THE MESSAGE

Wouldn't it be fun to be able to have conversations with animals?

communicate: (Kuh-MEW-nih-kate) to pass information along to each other

Cebus: (SEE-bus)

species: (SPEE-sheez) the same kind or type

In a way, you can. Even though animals don't speak with words, scientists who study animal behavior are beginning to understand how animals **communicate** through smells, sounds, touch, and body signals. Just what are they saying? Let's listen in. . . .

South American **Cebus** monkeys live in groups. As group members fan out in treetops to search for food, they call out to keep track of each other. Their calls are a way to say, "Hey, I'm over here." Individuals that become completely separated from the group use a louder call. It's like screaming, "Help! I'm lost. Where are you?"

Cebus monkeys call out to stay close together. But animals that prefer to live alone communicate to guard their space. Tigers mark out territories with scent sprayed from a special gland. Other tigers "read" this smell, which says, "No trespassing. Keep out."

Some messages also help creatures recognize one another.

The lights of fireflies—like sparks rising on dark summer nights—are how male fireflies say, "Look at me." Each male flashes his taillight in a special code to which only females of the same **species** respond. With hundreds of blinking lights in one area, this is how males are sure to find females of their own kind.

Mates must be able to recognize each other, too. Pairs of seabirds that nest in crowded neighborhoods know each other's calls.

In crowded living conditions, parents must also be able to pick out their young from among a field of babies. A nanny goat can. How? With her nose. Each mom has her baby's smell fixed in her mind.

Male white-throated sparrows even recognize the songs of neighbors. A stranger to the neighborhood with an unfamiliar song is chased away.

Most animals have ways to tell members of their own species that they don't

> IN THE PAST, GOD SPOKE TO OUR PEOPLE THROUGH THE PROPHETS. HE SPOKE AT MANY TIMES. HE SPOKE IN DIFFERENT WAYS. BUT IN THESE LAST DAYS, HE HAS SPOKEN TO US THROUGH HIS SON.
>
> HEBREWS 1:1–2a

Wanna dance? If you were a honeybee, you would. A worker bee that returns to the hive from gathering food does a waggle dance to tell bees where to find flowers. While dancing in a figure eight, the worker shakes her body and buzzes her wings. These signals, plus the length and direction of the dance, communicate the location of nectar and pollen.

want to fight. When two wolves greet, low-ranking members of the pack gently lick, nip, and smell the mouth of a **dominant** "top dog." The lower-ranked wolf is saying, "I know you're the boss. I don't want to fight."

Body language is also used by animals to keep playtimes from turning into fights. How do dogs say, "I want to play"? They plant their front paws and bow, resting on their elbows. Dogs have about thirty-five signals that keep fun times from turning into fights.

For safety, animals warn each other of emergencies. Alarm calls warn group members that predators are near. For the African **vervet** monkey, the alarm bark is one of at least five ways of yelling, "Danger! Danger!"

Animals *in* danger call out for help, too. When a baby elephant roars and screams, family members understand that it's saying, "Help!" and they come running. Ducklings and chicks peep to say, "I'm cold," or "I'm hungry."

Two thousand years ago, God had a message to communicate with us. So that we could understand what He had to say, He sent His message like a letter. Instead of paper and pen, though, God wrapped His words in flesh— in the form of a man—and sent Him into the world. That man was Jesus, the Word of God.

Jesus began His journey as a baby, in the home of a carpenter. When His family heard His first words, they had no idea that Jesus had spoken before—when He spoke and our world was created.

As an adult, Jesus revealed God's message through His life and miracles, as well as His words. In the end, Jesus allowed himself to be arrested, stripped, beaten, and mocked. Nails were driven into His hands and feet, and He was lifted high on a cross. The earth darkened and shook. In that darkness, God turned away from Jesus because we had turned away from God.

With arms open wide, Jesus said, "Father, forgive them—they don't know what they're doing." Then Jesus spoke one last time. "It is finished." A sword stabbed His side, and His life poured out. The Creator of the universe was buried in a tomb.

Three days later Jesus rose from the dead, and soon he

DOMINANT: (DAH-min-nent) the highest-ranking animal. It usually gets the first choice of food, mates, and nest sites.

vervet: (VER-vet)

returned to heaven. Then His message was spread by those who understood what God had communicated through Jesus. Two thousand years later, His message is still alive, carried inside all who have heard and believed.

What did God say through words wrapped in His Son?

"I love you. Turn from yourselves; come to me."

He's waiting for your answer. Have you run to Him?

Thought to remember:

God says "I love you" through Jesus.

Additional verses:

John 1:1–3, 14, 18; Romans 5:8;
2 Corinthians 3:3

CHECK IT OUT!

Become a pet detective. If you live with pets, check out how they talk to you and each other. In different situations:

How does it hold its body?

What does it do with its ears, eyes, lips, and tail? Its fur, nose, and voice?

How does it greet you?

How does it greet other animals?

Does your pet tell you when it wants to play? How?

How can you communicate with your pet that you want to play?

With pen and paper, record your pet's behavior. As you do, you will begin to understand what your pet is trying to communicate to those in its world.

DIG DEEPER!

★ how animals communicate

★ animals, talk

Also check individual names of animals.

6 THE MARVELS OF METAMORPHOSIS

It hatches from an egg, this worm with stubby legs.
It grows and grows and splits its skin
In the caterpillar stage.
But then it disappears inside a cozy case,
And it doesn't see the sun again
Until it is replaced.
Then it reappears, a butterfly—
New body and new face.

Most people would agree. The changes that butterflies go through as they grow from egg to adult are amazing. These changes are called **metamorphosis**, which means "change of form."

There are basically two types of metamorphosis: *incomplete* and *complete*.

Crickets, termites, and grasshoppers are a few of the insects that go through *incomplete* metamorphosis, which takes three stages to develop from egg to adult. First the egg hatches, and out crawls a creature called a **nymph.** These young insects look like tiny copies of their parents and usually eat the same food, but they have only itty-bitty buds for wings. Nymphs eat and grow until they *outgrow* their skin. Like a T-shirt that's too tight, their skin splits. Underneath is a new and bigger skin. Again, nymphs eat and grow until they outgrow *this* skin. With each split the nymph and its wings are a bit bigger. Finally, adults with full-sized wings break out of the skin, ready to have young of their own.

With incomplete metamorphosis, insects go through gradual change. Complete metamorphosis is different. . . .

Insects that go through complete metamorphosis—ants, bees, beetles, and butterflies—take *four* stages to develop from egg to adult.

First the egg hatches, and out crawls a creature called a **larva.** In the case of butterflies and moths, the larva is a caterpillar. It doesn't look anything at all like a but-

metamorphosis: (meh-tuh-MORE-fuh-sis)

nymph: (nimf)

The three stages of incomplete metamorphosis: egg→nymph→adult

larva: (LAR-vuh)

ANYONE WHO BELIEVES IN CHRIST IS A NEW CREATION. THE OLD IS GONE! THE NEW HAS COME! IT IS ALL FROM GOD. HE BROUGHT US BACK TO HIMSELF THROUGH CHRIST'S DEATH ON THE CROSS.

2 CORINTHIANS 5:17–18a

terfly, does it? The caterpillar eats and grows and eats and grows until it *outgrows* its skin. This happens several times. With each split, the caterpillar is bigger.

But to transform into a butterfly, the caterpillar must go through a third stage as a **pupa.** Inside a case of skin, the caterpillar body is broken down, and a butterfly body is built up. By the time the butterfly breaks free of its case as an adult, it's a completely new creature. It has a totally new body made for a totally new life.

pupa: (PYU-puh)

Another creature can go through complete metamorphosis—YOU! No, you don't curl up inside a pupa for weeks or months and then come out with a different body. You go through a *spiritual* metamorphosis. The moment we decide to follow Jesus, God takes away our old hearts and gives us completely new ones. As the butterfly has new physical life, we have new life inside—Jesus' life.

The four stages of complete metamorphosis: egg→larva→ pupa→adult

The caterpillar's body is made for a life of crawling among plants. It has simple eyes and stubby legs, and it chews on plants. But when the dainty butterfly breaks free of its case, it behaves like a butterfly instead of a caterpillar. It has large, compound eyes to see the world with and fine legs for balancing on flowers. A long, hollow tongue sips sweet nectar from the neck of blossoms. Instead of crawling among plants, it flutters from flower to flower on delicate wings.

When God gives us new hearts in Jesus, we also live differently than before. God gives us a fresh way to look at life. Our new hearts feed on God's love. We have the desire to follow Him. God transforms each of us from a caterpillar to a butterfly, from one who crawls to one who flies on the wings of an exciting new life.

Thought to remember:
I'm a butterfly. God made me a new person with a completely new heart.

Additional verses:
Galatians 2:20 (NIV); 6:15b; Colossians 3:3–4a; Ezekiel 36:26

Are you wondering where cocoons come into the picture? Most moth caterpillars spin cocoons around themselves when they're ready to pupate. This silken case protects the pupa while it develops into a moth. The single silk strand that silkworms spin their cocoons with is used as thread for fine clothing.

TRY IT!
Find a monarch caterpillar on a milkweed plant. Cut the plant at its base. Place it in a dish of water inside a large glass jar with a screen top. *Keep it out of the sun.* Replace wilted leaves with fresh ones from another milkweed plant.

Watch the caterpillar. How many times does it shed its skin? How does the pupa change? Make sure there is plenty of room in the container for the monarch to expand its wings when it emerges. Set it free as soon as its wings are dry.

Several companies sell kits that include a container, caterpillars, food, and instructions. These can be found on the Internet.

DIG DEEPER!
* insects
* insect metamorphosis
* butterflies and moths

7. Life-Giving Blood

Blood is something you probably don't like to talk about or see. Maybe it scares you or even makes you sick. That's normal. To most people blood means cuts, pain, and accidents.

To some animals, though, blood means food. As disgusting as this sounds, a blood-sucker's life depends on it. Most likely you've been the victim of a common bloodsucker, the mosquito. You know its annoying buzz, the itch of its bite.

Did you know that only *female* mosquitoes suck your blood? Normally, they eat plant nectar. But when it's time to lay eggs, a female must have blood for her eggs to develop. She searches for heat, sweat, and chemicals given off by your body.

Once she finds you, the mosquito sticks you with a "needle" on the end of a long mouthpart. She injects an **anticoagulant** that keeps your blood flowing. Two powerful pumps suck your blood. In less that two minutes, her fast-food meal is over!

Another common bloodsucker is the leech. Leeches lurk in dark waters and thick grass, waiting for you to pass by. Sensors on their bodies feel vibrations in water or on land. Eyespots detect shadows of passing prey. They're also sensitive to chemicals given off by animals.

Once leeches find you, how do they eat? Some leeches latch on to you with a mouth sucker, slicing through your skin with small teeth. Others stick you with a needlelike mouthpart to withdraw blood. Like that of mosquitoes, leech **saliva** has an anticoagulant. Another chemical in their saliva widens your blood vessel, so more blood flows. Leech saliva also numbs the nerves in your skin, so you don't even know they've joined you for dinner!

When it eats, a leech swells like a long balloon. One meal will satisfy it for about six months. Some leeches go as long as a year without eating.

If you live in South or Central America, you might not want to leave your window open at night. That's when vampire bats take to the air. This bat drinks the blood of sleeping pigs, cattle, sheep, birds, and humans. Its stomach can't digest anything solid.

To discover more about creatures that live off the lives of others, turn to "An Uninvited Guest" on page 118.

anticoagulant: (ant-eye-co-AG-u-lent) a substance that keeps blood from clotting

Not all leeches suck blood. Some eat worms, snails, and insect larvae.

saliva: (suh-LIE-va) the clear liquid in your mouth, also called spit

> CHRIST JESUS PAID THE PRICE TO SET US FREE. GOD GAVE HIM AS A SACRIFICE TO PAY FOR SINS. SO HE FORGIVES THE SINS OF THOSE WHO HAVE FAITH IN HIS BLOOD.
>
> ROMANS 3:24b–25

First, the sparrow-sized vampire bat lands near its prey. Hopping to the "dinner table," the bat sinks triangular teeth into the victim, scraping off a bit of skin. Just like with mosquitoes and leeches, vampire bat saliva keeps blood flowing. With lower lip pressed to the wound, the bat moves its tongue in and out to draw blood.

You can see how blood is life to these animals. Without it, mosquitoes, leeches, and vampire bats wouldn't survive.

As strange as it might sound, your life depends on someone else's blood, too. Jesus' blood is life to you. His blood brings you spiritual life.

RELATIONSHIP: (Ree-LAY-SHUN-SHIP) being related or connected to

All of us are born wanting to live life our own way instead of God's way. This attitude is called sin. It breaks our **relationship** with God, separating us from Him. In the Old Testament, God said that an animal's life is in its blood. The life of an animal—its blood—was needed to pay for sins, to heal our relationship with God.

Then Jesus came to this world. He was willing to give up His life to pay for our sins. His blood paid for our sins completely when He died on the cross. His blood is very special.

When we realize that our relationship with God is broken, and we believe that Jesus gave His blood for us, our separation from God is mended. We're forgiven and our spirits are given life—Jesus' life.

Thought to remember:
Jesus' blood paid for my sins.

Additional verses:
Leviticus 17:11; Ephesians 1:7; 2:13; Hebrews 9:12; 1 Peter 1:18–19

Most moths suck flower nectar through long feeding tubes. The vampire moth uses its feeding tube to suck the blood of victims. Little teeth on the tip and sides make it able to poke through skin.

FIND IT!

Mosquitoes need water to breed. They change into several forms as they grow:

egg→larva→pupa→adult

Can you find these in water near your home?

* Mosquito eggs float in clumps on stale water.
* Larvae look like small caterpillars that "hang" up and down in the water and wriggle when they swim.
* Pupae look like commas; they roll and bounce in the water.

DIG DEEPER!
* bloodsuckers
* mosquitoes
* leeches
* vampire bats

⑧ Whose Slave Are You?

How would you describe ants?

Bothersome little creatures that invite themselves to picnics? Tiny musclemen, able to lift many times their own weight? Would you call them hard workers?

Ants are known for being able to get a job done. But some species have come up with a strange way of getting out of work. How? To find out, shrink down to ant size.

From behind a clump of grass, watch a nearby ant colony. There's steady traffic in and out of the mound—workers delivering food, others carrying out dirt.

Then an ant scout scurries to an entrance. Moments later, excited workers pour from their home, hurrying down a trail of scent laid by the scout. You race over dead leaves and around rocks to keep up.

Soon the army of ants reaches another nest and surrounds it. When the defenders of this alien colony discover the attack, they try to escape with their young. But it's too late. The invaders block them, seizing their **brood**. When they've kidnapped as many larvae and pupae as can be carried, the ant invaders crawl home. The stolen young are eaten or raised to become slave workers of the slave-making ants. As adults, they have no idea that they're slaves. They perform the duties of a normal worker of the nest, including caring for more kidnapped young. But all this work helps only the family of master ants.

brood: (brewd)
the young of
an animal

> For we know that our old self was crucified with Him so that the body of sin might be done away with, that we should no longer be slaves to sin.
>
> ROMANS 6:6 (NIV)

Another amazing slave-maker is the Amazon ant. Unlike the first ants you visited, these large, shiny masters are dependent on their slaves. Worker Amazon ants have curved mouthparts, good only for piercing ant armor. Since they can't feed themselves, they spend their days in laziness, cleaning themselves or begging for food from slaves.

Watch as they raid other colonies, though. Mobs of Amazon workers swarm into alien nests, snatching brood before returning home. Any ant that gets in the way is killed by the Amazon's sharp mouthparts.

If Amazon ants aren't weird enough for you, visit the ant whose scientific name

ultimate: (UL-tim-et) the highest form. In this case, slave-making can't go any further.

means the "**ultimate**" ant. There are no workers in this slave-making species, only tiny queens and males. See if you can spot one of the queens—there it is, riding on the back of the **host** queen. The slave-maker queen has special claws to help her hang on to the slave queen, where she spends all her time. Born without a normal mouth, the slave-maker depends completely on slave workers for liquid food.

When the slave queen lays eggs, the master queen lays eggs, too. But the host's eggs develop only into workers. The slave-maker's eggs develop into queens and males. New queens fight for a position on the host queen's back. Losers must leave the nest to search for another host queen.

host: an animal or plant on which another animal or plant lives

Slave-making ants and their slaves? Sounds like something out of a science-fiction movie, doesn't it?! But they're real. Slavery can be real in our lives, too.

Have you ever stopped to think about what it's like to belong to somebody else? Slaves have no rights, no control over their own lives, no freedom. Before we became followers of Jesus, we were slaves to sin.

The first ants we visited had no idea they were slaves. We had no idea we were slaves, either. Sin was our way of life. But when we became tired of our sinful lives, we reached for Jesus to save us from our slavery. And He set us free.

How did He do that? The Bible says that "anyone who has died has been freed from sin" (Romans 6:7, NIV). When Jesus died, He took our old sinful selves with Him to the grave. By doing this, He freed us from our slave master, sin. Then, when Jesus rose again, we rose with Him. His life became ours. Because His life is pleasing to God, ours is, too.

Once we're freed from the power of sin, we're free to follow Jesus—free to live new lives!

Thought to remember:
Jesus' life sets me free from sin.

Additional verses:
Romans 6:7–8, 22; Galatians 2:20 (NIV); 5:1; John 8:35–36

Some slave-making ants spray a special scent to get inside the colonies they attack. This scent copies the odor that makes ants run away. When the defending ants smell it, they flee their nest. Ant invaders then get inside the nest without a fight.

PRETEND IT!
What would it be like to be a slave? See for yourself. Offer to be the slave of your mother or father. For a whole morning be willing to serve them and do any chores they ask. When you finish one task, report back to your master for another. Do only what they tell you to do. How would it feel to lose control over your life *forever*?

DIG DEEPER!
★ ants
★ slave-making ants

9 Cool It!

Pretend you're a lizard. What's the first thing you'd do when you jump out of bed in the morning?

For starters, you wouldn't *jump* out of bed. First you'd have to warm up.

Why?

Lizards are cold-blooded. Your body temperature changes with the temperature around you.

So first thing in the morning, crawl out onto a toasty rock. Flatten your body against it. Soak up some rays from the sun. Mmm. Feel the warmth.

Now that you're warm, streak across the earth like lightning. Snag those bugs. As your temperature rises from exercise and the heat of the day, turn to face the sun. That way less of your body is exposed to its blazing light. You can also hide in the shade of a bush. Or in your burrow, if necessary. Since you don't have sweat glands to cool off, you have to be careful not to overheat.

Like the lizard, all reptiles are cold-blooded. So are fish, insects, and amphibians.

Now pretend you're a dog. What's the first thing you do when you jump out of bed in the morning? Lick your master's feet to wake him? Fetch the newspaper or go on a walk? Any of these are possible. You don't have to wait for the day to heat up. You're ready to go.

To cool off when you take a walk, hang your tongue and pant. If you get too hot, sweat through the pads of your feet. Too cold? Shivering warms you up. In the winter, grow a thicker coat for **insulation**. In the summer, shed your winter coat all over your master's house.

Dogs, like all **mammals**, are warm-blooded. So are birds. Body temperatures are controlled from the inside—not the outside. An area in the brain keeps track of body temperature and regulates it. If the body is too cold, muscles are given the signal to contract. This causes shivering. Shivering creates heat.

Mammals and birds respond in different ways when they become too hot.

> It is God who works in you to will and to act according to His good purpose.
>
> PHILIPPIANS 2:13
> (NIV)

insulation:
(in-suh-LAY-
shun)

mammal:
(MAM-ul)
an animal that
has fur and
feeds its young
with milk

Humans and horses sweat. Dogs and birds pant. Pigs sweat through their feet, and elephants lose heat through their large ears. But both also use mud to stay comfortable.

Our body temperature isn't the only thing controlled from the inside out. So is our behavior. If we belong to Jesus, He's our temperature regulator. When we come to Jesus, He gives us a new heart, a heart that wants to obey God. His Spirit lives inside us, to teach and lead us. God works in us to please Him and carry out His will. As we go out into the world, Jesus keeps us steady. Then His life is expressed to those we come in contact with.

But God doesn't make us robots. Each day we have a choice to make. Either we choose to submit to God and walk in the Spirit, allowing His life to be shown through us. Or we choose to do our own thing. When we choose to do our own thing, we get a "high temperature." It shows that we're not following God. But just as our bodies work to keep our temperature under control, Jesus works to bring our spiritual temperature back to normal.

Every day we can yield to Jesus, our temperature regulator. He keeps us steady as we walk in this world!

Thought to remember:

I'm warm-blooded. Jesus is my temperature regulator.

Additional verses:

John 10:10b; Ezekiel 36:26; Hebrews 10:16; Isaiah 30:21; Galatians 5:16; Romans 6:13

The naked mole rat is an African mammal that lives in burrows. In one way this creature is more like a cold-blooded animal than a mammal. Its body temperature changes with surrounding temperatures. With no fur or fat to stay warm, and no sweat glands to cool off, how does it survive?

Temperatures inside burrows don't change much. The naked mole rat warms up near the surface. Then it snuggles with colony members to share its heat. Thin, loose skin keeps them from overheating.

TRY IT!

How does it feel to be a cold-blooded animal that hasn't warmed up? Fill a bowl with water and ice. Stick your hand in it for two minutes.

How does your hand feel when you bring it out? Is it hard to move? A cold-blooded animal moves slowly before its body warms up.

DIG DEEPER!

* cold-blooded animals
* warm-blooded animals
* how animals stay warm
* how animals keep cool

10 Got Roots?

H ere's a riddle:

I'm an anchor.
I'm usually unseen.
I feed plants—they can't live without me.
What am I?
I am a root.

Roots are the hidden feet of trees, grasses, and flowering plants. Because they grow unseen under *our* feet, we usually take little notice of them. But that doesn't make them any less important.

In fact, the first part to sprout out of a seed is the root. This first, **primary**, root immediately curves toward the earth and tunnels into the soil.

As the plant above the ground becomes larger, new root threads branch out from the sides of the primary root. These help anchor the plant and keep it from falling over. The network of roots below ground is usually as big as the network of stems and branches that we see aboveground.

Not only is the root system a foundation, but it feeds the plant, too. Near the root tips are thousands of fine root hairs that absorb water and **minerals**. The water and minerals travel to stems and leaves through a special system of tubes.

In order to keep up with the needs of a growing plant or tree, roots must also increase in size. They grow wider overall, but lengthen only at the tips. The very end of the tip is protected by a rounded root cap. As it snakes through gritty soil, this cap is crushed. When crushed, it gives off a liquid that helps the root slide through soil.

Most plants have one of two types of root systems. The first is called a taproot system. It's formed from a primary root that grows large and fleshy and stores food for

primary:
(PRY-mary)

mineral:
(MIN-er-ul)
a substance
found in nature
that's not plant
or animal.
Examples are
gold and salt.

"But I will bless any man who trusts in me. I will show my favor to the one who depends on me. He will be like a tree that is planted near water. It sends out its roots beside a stream. It is not afraid when heat comes. Its leaves are always green. It does not worry when there is no rain. It always bears fruit."

JEREMIAH 17:7-8

the plant. A few other roots sprout out of this fat central root that grows deep into the soil, but they're much smaller. Can you think of any plants that have taproots? Carrots, radishes, and beets do. When you eat these vegetables, you're eating taproots.

The **fibrous** root system is different from a taproot. Instead of one main carrot-shaped root, this network is made of many stringy roots that spread throughout the soil. You would have a hard time sorting the primary root from this mass of fibers that look like tangled hair. Can you think of plants that have fibrous root systems? Grasses do.

Here's another riddle:
I'm your anchor.
I'm unseen.
I feed your soul—you can't live without me.
Who am I?
I am God.

When we belong to Jesus, we are like trees. God is our root. He supports us. Without Him the problems of life could blow us over. But with God as our anchor, we can stand tall during stormy times.

God is also the very source of our lives; His life flows through us. Though we don't see Him, He feeds us and satisfies our thirst. He makes us grow.

A healthy tree depends on a large network of roots to reach food and water. Even though it has many large branches, this tree doesn't have to worry that its leaves will wilt or turn brown when the weather turns hot and dry. It will always bear fruit.

Like the tree that depends on a large network of roots, we depend on God. Even when the problems of life heat up, we don't have to worry. We can trust God to take care of all our needs. With God as our root, we can grow into strong, healthy trees.

Some roots begin *above*-ground, growing from stems. Tall corn plants get extra support from fingerlike roots that develop around the base of the stalk and reach down to the soil. Climbing roots also begin in stems. Their purpose is to fasten the plant to something solid as the plant climbs away from its base. You've probably seen ivy spread out on the side of a building, attached by climbing roots.

Coconuts may sprout wherever they fall. Unless these young trees are planted in deep holes, though, their roots will be shallow. Trees with shallow roots fall over more easily during storms.

DIG DEEPER!

* trees
* roots
* plants

CHECK IT OUT!

Find a dandelion. A dandelion has a large taproot that anchors it in the ground. Try pulling it out. What happens? Do the leaves break off? Now try digging out the dandelion with a shovel. How deep do its roots grow?

Next find a clump of wild grass. Grasses have fibrous roots that are much finer than a taproot. Try pulling out the clump. How well do the roots anchor the grass? Do some roots break off? Now dig around the plant with a shovel to loosen the soil. See if you can free all the roots. How many are there? How long are they?

Thought to remember:

God is my root.

Additional verses:

Colossians 2:6–7 (NIV); Romans 11:36 (NIV); 15:12–13; Revelation 22:16

11 All in the Family

In your imagination, take a walk around your neighborhood.
What kinds of life do you notice? At first you might just notice the big picture: grass, trees, and bushes. But as you continue, your list grows: dog, dandelion, butterfly, bee. An earthworm crawls at the edge of the sidewalk. A mushroom has sprouted beneath a tree. Then you hear a robin. *Then* you smell a skunk.

If you continued, your list would grow longer than an elm tree is tall. Nearly two million living things have been discovered living in, on, and above the earth. To organize and keep track of them all, each is sorted into groups with others similar to itself. The result looks something like a family tree.

The first branch is the kingdom. There are several kingdoms that separate simple living things from those that are more complicated. Plants and animals are separated into two different kingdoms.

Your pet dog belongs to—guess what? The animal kingdom. This large kingdom divides into two main branches: animals with backbones and animals without backbones.

> There is no Jew or Greek. There is no slave or free person. There is no male or female. Because you belong to Christ Jesus, you are all one.
>
> GALATIANS 3:28

Can you think of animals that *don't* have backbones? Are worms, spiders, sponges, starfish, or insects on your list? Now think of critters that have that bumpy line of bones running down their backs. Toads, tigers, and turkeys are a few. Dogs are in this group, too.

The branch of animals with backbones divides into five smaller branches. In which class does your dog belong?

COLD-BLOODED: having a body temperature that changes with surrounding air or water temperatures

We're **cold-blooded** and
We have gills to breathe underwater.
Our skin is covered with scales.
Most of us have fins and tails.
What are we?
Fish.

Test your mammal knowledge. What is the . . .
★ tallest mammal? The giraffe.
★ smallest mammal? The **pygmy** (PIG-me) shrew.
★ largest mammal? The whale.
★ largest *land* mammal? The elephant.
★ only mammal that can fly? The bat.

We're cold-blooded and
Our skin is thin and covered with slime.
When we're young we live in the water, and
As adults, most of us live on land.
What are we?
Amphibians.

We're cold-blooded and
Our skin is scaly and dry.
Our babies hatch from leathery eggs.
Some of us slither, some have four legs.
What are we?
Reptiles.

We're **warm-blooded** and
Our bodies are covered by feathers.
Our bones and beaks are light.
Most of us are made for flight.
What are we?
Birds.

We're warm-blooded and
We feed our babies with milk.
Our skin has fur or hair.
All of us breathe air.
What are we?
Mammals.

As you probably guessed, the dog is a mammal.

The mammal branch separates several more times. What does the dog have in common with cats, bears, and raccoons? It eats meat and has four legs.

When this group splits *again*, the dog is placed in a family with other doglike animals: wolves, coyotes, and foxes. And when *this* branch divides, only animals very closely related to dogs—wolves and coyotes—are included. The final split gives us the dog that lives in our homes.

Based on physical qualities, scientists have also placed humans on the animal family tree. We have backbones and we're mammals.

amphibian: (am-FIH-bee-un) frogs, toads, and salamanders

reptile: (REP-tile) snakes, lizards, turtles, and alligators

warm-blooded: having a body temperature that stays the same no matter what the surrounding temperatures are

mammal: (MAM-ul)

To discover more about cold- and warm-blooded animals, turn to "Cool It!" on page 28.

On the outside we may have similarities with animals. But on the inside we're different. We're made in God's image. Each of us has a spirit inside.

As humans, we can be divided into two groups—those who have God's spark of life in their spirits and those who don't.

Those who have God's spark of life in them have one thing in common: Jesus. When you have Jesus in common, it doesn't matter what color eyes, hair, or skin you have. It doesn't matter where you live, what language you speak, what kind of food you eat, or what kind of clothes you wear. All that matters is what you look like on the inside.

Belonging to Jesus makes you part of His family. You have brothers and sisters all over the world who also have Jesus in them.

Being a member of His family gives you a special bond with your brothers and sisters—even when you hardly know them. It's like coming home to someone who loves you. You're welcomed like family and made comfortable. You know you'll be taken care of. Praying for and helping each other makes the bond seem even stronger. Talking about Jesus with one another brings great joy!

Jesus knocks down the walls of our differences. He puts us together in a family and makes us close.

Thought to remember:

Belonging to Jesus makes me part of a special family.

Additional verses:

Genesis 1:27; 5:1; Galatians 4:6–7; Colossians 3:11; Ephesians 2:14

MATCH IT!

Match each animal with the group in which it fits.

fish	eagle
amphibian	poison-arrow frog
reptile	zebra
bird	cobra
mammal	shark
	eel
	porpoise
	penguin
	kangaroo
	crocodile
	bullfrog

The answers are on page 151.

DIG DEEPER!

* animal kingdom
* mammals
* birds
* fish
* amphibians
* reptiles

⑫ What's in a Name?

Do you know the story of Romeo and Juliet? They're a couple who fall in love but are separated by the hate between their families. Belonging to their families with their particular last names leads Juliet to cry out:

What's in a name? That which we call a rose
By any other name would smell as sweet.

—WILLIAM SHAKESPEARE

Sadly, Romeo and Juliet couldn't get beyond their names, because names are important.

So are ours. Think about your own. Do you know why your parents gave you your special name?

Maybe you were named after a relative or good friend. Maybe your name stands for something important. Or maybe your parents just liked the way it sounds.

Names help us stand out as individuals. They help people identify us. Nicknames can describe us. Last names show what family we belong to. Having a name is a lot better than being called "Hey, you!"

In the science world, names are important, too. So far, nearly two million living creatures have been discovered. Every year, the list grows. Each is given a **scientific** name. Like ours, these names are given carefully. They help avoid confusion. Here's why. . . .

Any living thing may have more than one common name. For example, a **domestic** dog is also called a canine, pooch, or puppy. The French word for dog is *chien*. In Spanish it's *perro*. The German name is *Hund*. If one scientist talks about a canine and another calls it a pooch or a perro, how can they be sure they're talking about the same thing?

They give it a scientific name. Dogs and all other liv-

> "She is going to have a son. You must give him the name Jesus. That is because he will save his people from their sins."
>
> MATTHEW 1:21

Scientific:
(sigh-en-TIF-ik)
having to do
with science

domestic
(duh-MESS-tik)

The two-name system used for living things today was invented by a Swedish man named Carl von Linn. The first, or **genus** (JEE-nus), name is given to closely related plants and animals. The second, or species, name sets apart the plant or animal from all others. The genus name is like your last name. It tells what family you belong to. The species name is like your first name. It identifies which individual you are in that family.

ing things have one official name based on the languages Latin and Greek. This name is recognized by scientists all over the world.

Canis familiaris:
(KAY-nis fuh-mil-
ee-YAIR-is)

Scientific names describe plants and animals. They give us clues about where they live or who discovered them. The name assigned to the dog you keep in your home is **Canis familiaris**. The word *Canis* comes from the Latin word that means—guess what? A dog. The second word, *familiaris*, comes from the Latin word that means it belongs to a household. It can also mean "familiar friend." That describes a domestic dog pretty well, doesn't it?

Lupus:
(LOO-pus)
Latrans:
(LAH-trans)

Scientific names are also used to distinguish between closely related plants and animals. The name for wolf is *Canis **lupus***. *Lupus* means "wolf." In the case of the coyote, *Canis **latrans***, the second name means "a barker."

Every living creature is given one scientific name that describes it.

God has given himself many names. Each one describes Him—they show us who He is and help us know and trust Him.

Here are a few.

Elohim:
(eh-LOW-heem)

The first Old Testament name used for God is **Elohim.** This name describes God as great and mighty. It tells us that God is one God yet three persons.

Jehovah:
(Jeh-HOE-vuh)

Another important Old Testament name is **Jehovah,** which means "I AM WHO I AM." It means that God wasn't created and has no beginning or end. Jehovah also means He reveals himself to us—to *you*. Wow!

Counselor:
(COWN-seh-ler)
someone who gives
advice

A few other names from the Old Testament are Creator, King, and Holy One. Isaiah 9:6 says that God is Wonderful and Mighty. It also calls Him **Counselor**, Everlasting Father, Prince of Peace. These names point out that God is the Holy Spirit, the Father, and Jesus.

The New Testament gives us a closeup view of Jesus Christ. Jesus means Savior. Christ means Messiah, the one chosen to come. Jesus is also called the Lamb of God, who takes away the sin of the world. He's the Son of Man, yet at the same time the Son of God.

When we crave meaning in our lives, Jesus is the Bread of Life, the Living Water. As the Way, the Truth, and the

Sometimes it's tough to live in this world. But we have an awesome God. In Him we have *everything* we need. These names may look a little tricky to pronounce, but they're so wonderful, it's worth it to give them a try.

❋ Jehovah-**jireh** (JIE-ruh) means "the Lord will provide." He takes care of our need for a Savior. He provides for all our needs with himself.

❋ Jehovah-**rapha** (RAH-fuh) means "the Lord heals." Healing is found in God.

❋ Jehovah-**nissi** (NEE-see) means "the Lord our banner." God goes to bat for us.

❋ Jehovah-**Shalom** (shaw-LOAM) means "the Lord our peace." We are at peace with God because of Jesus. As a result, we have peace in our hearts.

❋ Jehovah-**roeh** (ROW-eh) means "the Lord my shepherd." God watches over us.

❋ Jehovah-**tsidkenu** (tsid-KEH-new) means "the Lord our righteousness." We don't have to try to be righteous. Jesus is righteous for us.

❋ Jehovah-**shammah** (SHAW-mah) means "the Lord is present." God is always with us. He never deserts us.

FIND IT!

Find more names of God in this word puzzle. As you read each one, pause to let its meaning soak in. Names are forward, backward, up, down, and diagonal.

A NAME NO ONE KNOWS BUT HIMSELF	FAITHFUL	ONE AND ONLY
	FATHER	
BEGINNING	GOD ABOVE ALL GODS	SAVIOR
COMFORTER		FIRST
	JUDGE	LAST
CREATOR	LORD	TRUE
END	MORNING STAR	WORD OF GOD

```
G O D A B O V E A L L G O D S
A N M O R N I N G S T A R D P
N E G S G B F A Q L Y C V S J
A A N I A F T A X X W O K U E
M N I D L V O S T Z U P D O L
E D N I A M I D L H R G G D U
N O N C O M F O R T E R K S F
O N I I D X R F R O U R T B H
O L G S L D K I W J W Y T U T
N Y E V R A C R O T A E R C I
E Z B N S U S S D M T P U A A
K N O W S B U T H I M S E L F
```

The answers are on page 151.

DIG DEEPER!

✦ Latin names
✦ scientific names

Life, He brings us to eternal life. Then He becomes the Good Shepherd because He takes care of us. The Holy Spirit lives inside us and comforts us. God becomes our Father.

Because God is the One and Only, the Almighty, King of Kings and Lord of Lords, we honor Him above all else on earth. We look at Him with awe. We worship Him.

Who is God? These names give us a glimpse. As we watch for His names in the Bible, we can discover more about the One who calls us by name!

Thought to remember:
God reveals himself to me by His names.

Additional verses:
Isaiah 42:8a; John 1:1, 14; Mathew 16:13–16; Philippians 2:8–10; Psalm 34:3 (NIV); Isaiah 43:1; Acts 11:26

⟨13⟩ Fantastic Fathers

What do Darwin's frogs, sea horses, and three-spined sticklebacks have in common?

The males of these animals are fantastic fathers.

In the animal world, most babies hatch out of eggs that are laid and left on their own. Some babies are cared for by their mothers. Only a few are cared for by their dads alone. The male Darwin's frog of South America is one of these superduper dads. His fatherhood begins when a female frog lays her eggs on the ground. The male guards the eggs from **predators** until they're almost ready to hatch. Then he snatches up the eggs with his tongue, slipping them through a slit in his mouth and into his vocal sac. Here—within the safety of a pouch— the tadpoles hatch and transform into adults. When fully developed, the tiny frogs with pointed snouts hop from their dark world to begin life on their own.

Another first-class father is the male sea horse. This spiny fish with the horselike head has a brood pouch on his lower stomach. A female squirts her eggs into this pouch through an egg-laying tube, then swims away. Safe, and fed by liquid food inside their father's soft pouch, the eggs develop. A few weeks later, the baby sea horses are big enough to leave this cozy nest. Their father wraps his tail around a strand of seaweed and squeezes out hundreds of babies, one by one. They'll grow anchored to underwater plants until they're as big as their parents, ready to have babies themselves.

The three-spined stickleback is also a dazzling dad. This fish's fatherly chores begin as he builds a nest for his young. In the shallow waters of lakes and ponds, he clears a sandy pit with his bottom fins. For several days the three-spined stickleback gathers bits of algae and plants, shaping these into an oblong mound. When finished, he swims back and forth over the top, releasing a "glue" to hold his nest together. The final touch is made when he swims through the middle to form a tunnel.

Once the male convinces a female to lay her eggs in his nest, he fertilizes them. Then he's on his own to protect the eggs from predators, fan them with fresh water,

Predator: (PREH-duh-ter) an animal that hunts other animals for food

To discover more about how animals care for their young, turn to "Worth the Trouble" on page 43.

> Because you are his children, God sent the Spirit of his Son into our hearts. He is the Holy Spirit. By his power we call God "Abba." Abba means Father.
>
> GALATIANS 4:6

What about me? Sometimes life doesn't seem fair. Maybe you don't have an earthly father. Or if you do, maybe he lives far away or just isn't there for you. God understands how this leaves an empty space as big as the sky inside you. He wants to fill that empty space. He calls himself "a father to the fatherless." Run to His arms. He will be your dad.

WRITE IT!

When you're by yourself, write a letter to God the Father. Pour out your heart to Him. Tell Him your dreams and hopes, and about the things that bother you, too. Tell Him you love Him. You don't ever have to worry about what He'll think about you. You can be yourself, because He made you and knows you through and through. Sign the letter with your name.

DIG DEEPER!

* animal dads
* animal fathers
* animal parents
* sea horses
* frogs
* amphibians

and make repairs. He even removes eggs that die.

Two weeks later, the eggs hatch. But the father's duties aren't over yet. His babies live together for a few more days inside their nursery. If they wander away, he catches them in his mouth and spits them out in the safety of his home.

These fathers give us a glimmer of what it means to be a dad. They protect and care for their young until they're ready to live on their own. But an important ingredient is missing. Can you guess what it is?

Love.

Human fathers love their children. God the Father loves His children, too. In fact, His love for us is so great that He was even willing to give up His own Son so that we could be His children.

This is the kind of Father He is:

* He's always with you, even though you can't see Him. God isn't a faraway Father, somewhere off in heaven where you can't reach Him (see John 17:21–23, NIV).

* He promises that He'll never leave you. Nothing can separate you from His love (see Hebrews 13:5; Romans 8:38).

* He always has time for you and is ready to listen (see Psalm 94:9).

* He understands you completely (see Hebrews 4:15).

* He's kind, gentle, and patient (see 1 John 4:16; 1 Corinthians 13:4–8).

* He protects you as no one else can because He's greater than anything else in the universe (see Psalm 91:1–4).

* He disciplines you with tenderness (see Hebrews 12:6, NIV).

* He cheers and roots for you! (see Romans 8:31).

What a dad to have on your side! Climb onto His lap. Lay your head on His shoulder. Tell Him your fears and worries. Tell Him the things you're glad about, too.

Thought to remember:
God is my Father.

Additional verses:
John 14:6; Romans 8:15–17a, 38–39; Psalm 68:5 (NIV); 27:10

14 WHO NEEDS PARENTS?

Wouldn't it be a strange world if humans were born able to talk, walk, and feed themselves?

Many animals are. But some are more like humans—born helpless, they must be cared for by their parents. Animal babies arrive in this world in different stages of development. Sooner or later, though, all become independent from their parents.

Some babies need no help from their parents at all. In fact, they may not even see their parents—ever. Can you stop for a minute and think of some? Did fish come to mind? Snakes? Insects? Most fish, snakes, and insects hatch from eggs, ready to go. Animals that are born fully able to take care of themselves are called **precocial.** Ducks, pheasants, and ostriches peck out of their eggs with eyes open. They are covered with fuzz, ready to run around, and able to feed themselves. Ducklings can even swim, but they can't fly. These creatures still depend on parents to help them find food and to provide protection.

Guinea pigs, zebras, and horses are also well developed at birth. So are elephants. After growing for nearly two years inside mama's belly, elephant calves stand soon after coming into this world. Within an hour these 250-pound babies join the herd. Keeping up with the herd provides protection from predators. But elephant babies take about twelve years to become young adults.

Unlike elephants, many animals are not up and running at birth. Can you think of some that live in our homes? How about puppies and kittens? Robins begin life in this world blind, naked, and unable to move about in nests. They are totally dependent on parents for food and warmth. Helpless babies are called **altricial**. Kangaroo babies—or joeys—win the prize for being undeveloped. Naked, blind, and deaf, a joey is less than an inch long at birth. This bean-sized baby then

Precocial (Pre-CO-shul)

altricial (al-TRIH-shul)

> But grow in the grace and knowledge of our Lord and Savior Jesus Christ. To him be glory both now and forever! Amen.
>
> 2 PETER 3:18 (NIV)

Elephants are able to walk soon after birth, but they have to learn to use their trunks. At first the baby swings it back and forth and in circles. After a few weeks the elephant starts to pick up small items but can't quite get them to its mouth. About a year goes by before the baby learns to control all fifty thousand muscles in its trunk.

NAME IT!

Use the code to unscramble the names of different animal babies.

a	b	c	d	e	f	g	h	i
1	2	3	4	5	6	7	8	9

j	k	l	m	n	o	p	q	r
10	11	12	13	14	15	16	17	18

s	t	u	v	w	x	y	z
19	20	21	22	23	24	25	26

chicken: 3 8 9 3 11

goat: 11 9 4

porcupine: 16 15 18 3 21 16 5 20 20 5

elk: 3 1 12 6

goose: 7 15 19 12 9 14 7

fish: 6 18 25

eel: 5 12 22 5 18

sheep: 12 1 13 2

seal: 16 21 16

zebra: 6 15 1 12

lion: 3 21 2

llama: 3 18 9 1

kangaroo: 10 15 5 25

skunk: 11 9 20

The answers are on page 152.

DIG DEEPER!

* animal babies
* animals, young
* kangaroos
* elephants
* birds

squirms about six inches through the mother's fur to her warm pouch. Once safely inside, it clamps onto a nipple to drink milk for about three months while it grows.

After about six months inside its mother's pouch, a young kangaroo's eyes and ears are developed, and it has fur. Slowly it spends more time in the world eating grass, returning to the pouch for comfort, safety, and sips of milk. By a year-and-a-half, the joey is ready for independent life.

As you might guess, humans are also altricial. At first we can't walk or talk, and can't see very well. We must be bathed, fed milk, and kept warm by our parents. As we develop, our teeth come in and we're able to eat solid food. We take our first steps. Sounds become words, and words become sentences. Slowly we do more on our own, apart from our parents. Nearly twenty years pass before we're independent adults.

Humans need time to mature physically. But how do humans mature spiritually? Are we precocial or altricial?

Both. When we're born into the family of God, we have everything in Jesus that we need for life. But as newborn babies in Christ, we need God, our Father, to take care of us. He feeds us spiritual milk; slowly we begin to understand all that Jesus has done for us. As we grow up in Christ, we take our first steps in the Spirit and learn to walk with God. The fruit of the Spirit is displayed in our lives. We learn how to love others. When there are problems in our lives and we see how God takes care of them, we also learn that we can trust Him. Our understanding of His care for us grows. Knowing and loving the Lord brings more and more joy.

Our lives are spent learning all that Jesus has already done for us. But instead of growing *independent* from God, we grow more dependent on Him.

Thought to remember:

As I mature in Jesus, I will depend on Him more.

Additional verses:

2 Peter 1:3; James 1:2–4 (NIV); Ephesians 4:11–15

⑮ WORTH the TROUBLE

As the shadow of winter creeps across Antarctica, it brings an icy blanket of cold and snow, harsh winds, and almost endless darkness. At a time when most animals escape to friendlier lands, the emperor penguin settles in. Penguin couples mate, the female lays one grapefruit-sized egg, and then she leaves to feed. It's the father's job to hatch the egg. For two months the male stands as still as a soldier, braving bitter temperatures with an egg tucked between his body and the tops of his toasty toes.

The female takes over when she returns. For two more months the chick snuggles inside the warm, safe pouch of fat and fur just above its mother's feet.

Is one chick worth all this trouble? For the penguin parents it is. Because they lay only one egg at a time, they spend a lot of time and energy to make sure that baby hatches, lives, and has children of its own. Penguins aren't like many creatures that lay hundreds, thousands, or even *millions* of unprotected eggs at a time. Only a few of those eggs survive predators, disease, and bad weather.

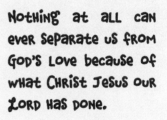

Nothing at all can ever separate us from God's love because of what Christ Jesus our Lord has done.

ROMANS 8:39b

What other animals keep their young close to protect them?

The sand grouse does. This mother bird spreads her wings to shelter her young. Some fish parents gather their young in their mouths and hide them there until danger passes.

Scorpions keep their babies close, too. Baby scorpions hatch on top of their mama's back and then ride piggyback until ready to live on their own. A scorpion that keeps its babies nearby says to the world: "You mess with my babies and you'll have to mess with the stinger on my tail!"

Wolf spiders have a similar arrangement. The female carries her egg sac until spiderlings hatch. Then, like the scorpion, baby wolf spiders hitch a ride on their mother's back.

Several water birds do the same. Swans, **grebes**, flamingos, and **loons** carry fuzzy chicks on their backs while they swim. Nestled under a parent's wings, these chicks sleep in safety, warm and dry.

grebe: (Greeb) a diving bird with short wings and a short tail

loon: (rhymes with moon) a diving bird with a pointed beak. Larger than grebes.

Can you think of other ways animals keep their young close? How about kangaroos, koalas, and opossums? Their babies develop in pouches. An opossum baby rides its mama's back once it's out of the pouch. When a koala emerges, it clings to its mother's neck.

THINK ABOUT IT!

What's it like to keep another living thing close at all times? See for yourself. Find a doll or stuffed animal and carry it around for three hours. During this time you can lay your "baby" on your lap, but you must never set it aside. When your three hours are up, *think about it*:

1) How does holding a baby for three hours change your activities?

2) What would it be like taking care of a baby for a whole day? A week? A month? God holds you close your whole life!

DIG DEEPER

* animals and their babies
* animal parents
* how animals care for their young

Chimpanzees and gorillas also keep their infants close. At birth, these babies are held snug against their mother's chest, supported by her arm. When strong enough, they clutch their mama's stomach hair. But as they grow and are able to hold on tight, chimps and gorillas ride like a jockey on a horse.

During rainstorms, chimp and gorilla mothers wrap their babies in their arms and lean forward to keep them dry. When attacked, a chimp mother crouches over her offspring to protect it. A South American monkey also huddles over his young to shelter them from storms and danger.

In a similar way, each of us who belongs to Jesus is kept close to Him. God doesn't bring us into His family to leave us on our own or forget about us. Like the penguin chick that is sheltered on its parents' feet for months, each of us is worth it. God made us. He paid an expensive price—His Son, Jesus—to make us His children.

How does God keep us close?

Just as the sand grouse shelters her young under her wings, God hides us under the safety of His wings.

Just as the chimp cradles her baby, the Good Shepherd carries us—His lambs—in His gentle arms, close to His heart.

And just as some fish hold their young in the safest place possible—their mouths—God holds us in the safest place we could be. God the Father holds us in His hand. There isn't any place safer than His hand, because there's no one greater than He is. We can't be snatched away from the safety of our Father's grasp.

On this earth, there's always a chance that we can be separated from those we love. But we can be sure that nothing will ever separate us from God's love. We can count on Him to keep us secure—to hold us close to Him.

Thought to remember:

God holds me close. I can't be snatched away from the safety of His arms.

Additional verses:

Psalm 36:7; 91:4; Isaiah 40:11; 46:3b–4; 49:15–16; John 10:27–29; Romans 8:38–39

If someone asked if you're afraid of being eaten by a plant, you'd say, "No way! That only happens in movies."

That's true.

Unless you're a bug.

Then you'd better watch where you step or where you fly, because there are over five hundred species of animal-eating plants. These **carnivorous** plants eat ants, flies, beetles, mosquitoes, and butterflies. Every now and then some even trap larger food—frogs and rats and small birds.

carnivorous:
(car-NIHV-
or-us)
meat eating

This is how they work.

Imagine you're a hungry fly. The red mouth of a Venus flytrap looks inviting. Smells sweet, too. You glide into the mouth, but without knowing it, you touch tiny trigger hairs. The jaws of this plant snap shut! Unless you're a *very* small fly that can crawl between the teeth of this prison, you are stuck. Squirming only makes the jaws squeeze harder. Liquid fills the mouth, drowning you.

> We love because He loved us first.
>
> 1 JOHN 4:19

Or suppose the bright, sweet-smelling pitcher plant invites you in. You land on the hood that hangs over the wide mouth of this trumpet-shaped leaf. Mmm. The nectar at the mouth smells even sweeter. There's a pool at the bottom of this leaf, but not to worry. You'll just stand on the lip of the mouth and reach inside for the nectar. Oops, this leaf is waxy. You slide to the hairs below. It's okay, don't panic. You'll use these long hairs to climb out. Uh-oh. No, you won't. These hairs all point down. There's only one way to go—down to the pool where you will drown.

Now suppose you're a thirsty fly. Dewdrops sparkle like rubies on the ends of long stalks that grow out of sundew plant leaves. Mmm. They smell *so* sweet. You glide in for a drink, and your wing touches one of the dewdrops. Surprise! These dewdrops aren't water, they're glue. Your wing is stuck. You squirm, but your foot and other wing get stuck, too. Now the stalks begin to fold toward the leaf, pinning you to the plant. Dinner has begun.

Venus flytraps, pitcher plants, and sundews trap their food in different ways, but they're also similar. Carnivorous plants live in places that have poor soil. By trapping

A few creatures live inside pitcher plants without being harmed. Some spiders weave webs at the mouths of pitcher plants. They drop to the pools on silk strands to steal victims.

One type of mosquito lays eggs in the pool. These hatch into larvae that eat the dead bugs in this death trap. They live in the pitcher plant's juices until they become adults and fly away.

GROW IT!

Venus flytraps and sundews can be bought in grocery stores, local greenhouses, and from the Internet. Try these experiments:

1) Does the Venus flytrap close if only one of the trigger hairs is touched?

2) Does your Venus flytrap react more strongly to dead or living bugs?

3) What happens when you feed a carnivorous plant other "foods" such as leaves, a bit of ground beef, or bread?

DIG DEEPER!

* carnivorous plants
* meat-eating plants
* Venus flytraps
* sundews

bugs, these plants get the food they need to grow bigger and stronger. They use sweet-smelling nectar to lure their prey. And they all have **digestive juices** that go to work as soon as a victim is caught.

It's a relief to know there are no *man*-eating plants around, isn't it?!

But there's another kind of trap that can snare us. That trap is the belief that we need to do things to get God to love and accept us. When we think this way, we struggle like a fly stuck in the Venus flytrap. Because we could never know when enough is enough, we tire ourselves by doing more and more and more. Our energy is sucked out.

The truth is, God already thinks a lot of you. Here are a few of the things He says about you:

* "You are my child. This is true of you because you were born into My family, not because of anything you did" (see John 1:12).

* "Because you're in my family, I accept you just the way you are. You don't have to be perfect" (see 2 Corinthians 5:21).

* "There's no one who can **condemn** you, because I don't" (see Romans 8:1, NIV).

* "I love you" (see 1 John 4:10).

While Jesus was here on earth, the miracles He performed didn't make Him God. He performed miracles *because* He was God. It's the same for us. The things we do for God don't make Him love us more. Each of us is valuable because of who we are, not what we do.

And that's a relief!

Thought to remember:

What I do comes out of who I am in Jesus.

Additional verses:

1 John 4:10; Galatians 3:3; 3:26; Ephesians 1:4–5; Romans 8:1 (NIV); 5:1; Psalm 139:13–14

digestive juices: (die-JES-tiv JOOS-ez) Liquids that help break down food so it can be used by the body

condemn: (cun-DEM) to pass judgment against someone

47 Don't Be Fooled

Try this multiple-choice question just for fun:

A copycat is

a) a cat who copies your homework

b) someone who copies the behavior of someone else

c) the name for monks who copied the Bible in the Middle Ages

d) all of the above

If you guessed "a" or "c" or "d," you have a wonderful imagination! If you guessed "b," give yourself a gold star. Copycats *are* people who take on the looks or behavior of someone else. Did you know that some animals are copycats, too? They **mimic** other animals.

mimic: (MIM-ick)

Do they do this for fun?

mimicry: (MIM-ick-ree)

For some animals, **mimicry** is a matter of life and death. The red-spotted purple butterfly of North America is a good example.

> His sheep follow him because they know his voice.
>
> JOHN 10:4b

fore wings: the upper wings of a four-winged insect

This butterfly has black **fore wings** and blue **hind wings**. Its **under wings** are decorated with orange spots. Red-spotted purples (let's call them RSPs for short) are copycats of another butterfly, the pipe-vine swallowtail. These swallowtails also have dark fore wings, blue hind wings, and orange spots on their under wings. Why do RSPs mimic pipe-vine swallowtails?

hind wings: the lower wings of a four-winged insect

The caterpillars of pipe-vine swallowtail butterflies feast on the pipe vine, a poisonous plant with heart-shaped leaves. The poison of this plant is carried through to the butterfly after metamorphosis. One taste is enough to teach a bird that the black-and-blue wing pattern means "WARNING! WARNING! DO NOT EAT!"

under wings: the surface seen when wings are closed

The RSP is harmless. But because it lives in the same area as the pipe-vine swallowtail, has the same coloration, and is about the same size, predators steer clear.

Yellow and black stripes protect other insect look-alikes that mimic wasps, honeybees, and yellow jackets. The hover fly is one of them. Not only are its yellow and black stripes patterned like a wasp's, but its body is shaped like a wasp, too. A bird that's been stung by a wasp will also avoid a hover fly, even though the fly is harmless—it has no stinger. Maybe you've been fooled by a copycat fly, too.

Mimicry also occurs in fish. The moray eel has a distinct eye and is freckled with light-colored spots. This dangerous eel lives among rocks and coral. It's mimicked by a harmless fish that spreads a fin on its back to display a large spot that looks like the eel's eye. It becomes a look-alike of the moray eel, and predators scatter.

EXPLORE IT!

Ask your parents to take you to a department store. Look for the following and compare:

* real and fake diamonds
* a real and a fake leather coat or sofa
* a real and a fake fur coat

It's hard to tell the fake from the real, isn't it? Even when you look closely, it can be hard to tell the difference. See how easy it would be for an animal to be fooled by the bright colors and patterns of a mimic?

DIG DEEPER!

* mimicry
* animal disguises
* animal behavior
* butterflies

Mimicry also occurs in birds. One of the strangest examples is the cuckoo bird. Through mimicry it tricks other birds into raising its young. While one bird—the redstart—is away from its nest, the female cuckoo sneaks in to lay an egg. The redstart is fooled into taking care of the cuckoo's egg and baby because the cuckoo's blue egg is a copycat of the redstart's egg.

Some baby cuckoos push the babies of their foster parents out of the nest. They may look like and imitate their hosts' babies, too.

Mimicry works because animals are fooled into believing that an insect, bird, or egg is something other than what it really is. There's also a type of mimicry that goes on in our thoughts. It happens when our enemy, Satan, tries to trick us into believing things about ourselves that aren't true.

Maybe you've had thoughts such as *I'm stupid. I'm ugly. Nobody likes me. I'm not good enough for God to love.* Think about how these thoughts sound. Do they sound just like your own voice?

Satan wants to hurt us. If he gave you thoughts that sounded like someone other than yourself, you wouldn't believe them. So he mimics your voice to make the bad thoughts seem as if they're coming from inside your own head. Then you're more likely to accept them—just as the redstart accepts cuckoos' eggs.

You don't need to be afraid of Satan—Jesus conquered Satan when He died on the cross and rose from the dead. But you do need to recognize when he's trying to discourage you. Then you won't listen to his harmful messages.

Telling the difference is simple. We know God's voice because He's the Good Shepherd and we're His sheep. The Shepherd takes special care of us. He only tells us things to help us.

On the other hand, Satan is like a butcher to sheep—he's out to deceive and destroy. So when we get thoughts that make us feel bad about ourselves, we know where they're coming from. Then we can turn to Jesus for protection. We can tell Satan we belong to Jesus, to leave us alone.

You don't have to listen to the enemy's bad thoughts. Don't be fooled.

Thought to remember:

Don't be fooled. Recognize where your thoughts are coming from.

Additional verses:

John 10:7–11; Psalm 95:7; Hebrews 2:14; James 4:7

18 Squeaky Clean

Give these riddles a try:

What do you call a muddy duck?
A foul fowl.

What do you call a dirty dog?
A shabby dog.

What do you call a sloppy rodent?
A ratty rat.

When was the last time you saw a foul fowl, shabby dog, or ratty rat? You may have seen a shabby dog because its owner didn't take care of it. But unclean animals are rare. There's a reason for that.

Being unclean is unhealthy. It leads to problems such as disease and **parasites**—even death.

Healthy feathers are important to birds that fly to find food or that must take off quickly to escape danger. To keep feathers in tip-top shape, birds bathe in water. Then they **preen.** Each feather is made of thin strands with tiny hooks. Sometimes these hooks separate. A bird draws the strands through its beak to put the feather back together again—like a zipper being zipped.

> But the kindness and love of God our Savior appeared. He saved us. It wasn't because of the good things we had done. It was because of His mercy. He saved us by washing away our sins. We were born again. The Holy Spirit gave us new life.
>
> TITUS 3:4–5

While preening, the bird removes dirt and rearranges feathers. Reaching to a gland at its lower back, the bird collects preening oil to spread through its feathers. How does oil keep feathers healthy? Like shoe polish on shoes, oil cleans feathers and keeps them moist and flexible. Oil also waterproofs feathers to keep birds warm and dry.

Birds bathe and preen to keep their feathers clean. What about animals with fur?

If you have dogs, cats, or rabbits, you've seen them lick themselves clean. Cats—and even some dogs—wet their paws to wipe their faces.

Chimpanzees don't lick themselves to stay squeaky clean. These small apes **groom**

To discover
more about
feathers, turn
to "Born to
Fly" on page
58.

Birds called jays have a strange way of keeping clean. They crush ants with their bills and spread ant body juices throughout their feathers. Ant "soap" is believed to kill lice, a parasite that lives on birds.

To discover more about other animal helpers, turn to "Positive Partnerships" on page 115.

their bodies. Spreading hairs apart with the fingers of one hand, they pluck out bits of dry skin, dirt, ticks, and lice with the other. For those hard-to-reach places—back, rump, and head—chimps groom each other. They also use sticks to pick their teeth. Leaves are used like tissue to wipe away dirt, mucous, and blood.

Fish don't have fingers, and they can't lick their bodies, either. So how do they stay spotless? Some go to the cleaners! Cleaner fish and shrimp eat parasites and bits of dead skin off their visitors. Birds called oxpeckers do the same for zebras, buffalo, and other African animals.

Elephants love to bathe in water. But they also take dust baths. These beasts spray dust on themselves with their trunks. Dust acts as bug repellent and sunscreen for elephants' nearly hairless skin. Another way to condition skin is to **wallow** in cool mud. Like dust, mud blocks sunrays and gets rid of pesky parasites. Imagine your parents' reaction if you told them you wanted to take a dust or mud bath!

wallow: (WAH-low) to wiggle and roll around in mud

Of course, keeping clean is just as important for our health, too. When we're careless about keeping clean, our friends don't want to come too close! Soap and water take care of the outside of our bodies.

But what about the inside, where our spirit lives? The Old Testament talks about needing to be cleansed from sin. Sin makes us dirty on the inside so that we can't come close to God. Being separated from God makes our hearts feel guilty and empty. Can soap and water wash our hearts, too?

For sin we need something much more powerful than soap and water. Like the chimp who needs another to groom those hard-to-reach places, we need Jesus to cleanse our "heart"-to-reach place. There's only one thing that can scrub the stain of sin from our hearts—Jesus' blood.

How can we bathe our hearts in His *blood*? Simply by believing that Jesus offered His lifeblood on the cross for us. The moment we believe, He gives us new hearts, as fresh and clean as white snow. With spotless hearts, we're free from guilt. Then we can come near to God.

But even with new hearts, we can still choose to jump in the mud puddles of sin. Then what do we do? It's simple. We admit to God what we've done. Sometimes that's hard to do, because there are times when we don't like to admit that we've been wrong. But God is kind and tender. When we tell Him we're wrong, He's always ready to forgive.

Soap and water are important for our physical health. Jesus' blood is important for our spiritual health. Have you gone to Jesus to become squeaky clean?

Thought to remember:

Jesus makes my heart clean.

Additional verses:

Psalm 51:2; Jeremiah 33:8; Isaiah 1:18; Ezekiel 36:26; Hebrews 9:14; 1 John 1:7, 9

TRY IT!

For this activity all you need is a feather. If you don't have one lying around the house, you might find one outside wherever birds gather. Or buy one at a local craft store. Hold the feather between your fingers. Separate the strands that make up the colored part of the feather. To zip them together again, press the separated halves together. Then run your pointer finger and thumb from the base of the strands to the tips. Do the separated halves stick together again? When a bird preens, it makes sure all the strands are zipped together.

DIG DEEPER!

* how animals keep clean
* ducks
* elephants
* fish
* animal comfort behavior
* animal behavior

19 1+1=1

W hat does one plus one equal?

It's simple. If you have one rose plant, and you set another rose plant next to it, you now have two plants.

But there's a case when one plus one doesn't equal two. If you have one rose plant and *join* another to it, you still have only one plant.

Perhaps you're wondering if it's really possible to unite one plant to another. Yes, it is—by a process called **grafting.** Grafting is a way of producing a new plant by bringing two plant parts together. It's often done on woody plants such as trees, shrubs, roses, and grapevines. The result is a plant that's not usually found in nature.

grafting: (GRAFT-ing)

Suppose you have a rose plant with flashy red blossoms, but it doesn't resist disease very well. You could graft it into a sturdy rose that is more disease resistant. Then you'd get the best of both worlds. In this case the sturdy disease-resistant rose will be the base plant in the graft. It's called the stock, or rootstock. As the lower part of the graft, the stock becomes the new plant's root system. A shoot from the rose plant with flashy flowers is grafted into the rootstock. It's called the **scion.**

Scion: (SY-un)

> "I am the vine. You are the branches."
>
> JOHN 15:5a

How does a graft work? Inside the bark is a layer of cells called the **cambium.** It's the layer of growing tissue in woody plants. When the cambium cells of both stock and scion are lined up, they form a network of tubes that carry food and water throughout both plants. The tubes of both plants grow together and the plants bond—to become one plant.

cambium: (CAM-be-um)

Several methods are used to bring two plants together. In all of them, the two cambium layers must meet. Depending on which method is used, the layers may have to be tied or taped together. A coat of wax seals moisture in and disease out.

Why do gardeners join plants? For many reasons. The flashy, delicate rose that's grafted into the sturdy rootstock is one example. The strengths of the rootstock are carried into the scion.

Or suppose you have an apple tree with sour fruit. You could graft scions from a tree with sweet fruit onto it. Several types of apples can be grafted onto one tree. Grafts are also used to reproduce certain plants. They're made to improve the shape, size, and timing of fruit, and to repair injured trees. They're also made for fun.

Grafting isn't only performed on plants. Surgeons may graft skin, nerves, and bones from one part of a person's body onto an injured part. Grafting also takes place in our spirits. It describes our relationship with Jesus.

Before we belong to Jesus, we're separate from Him. But when we believe in Jesus to save us from our sins, we're grafted permanently into Him. We become one of His branches, grafted into the Tree of Life. He's the rootstock, and we're the scions. Just as two grafted plants are joined to become one, so are we.

Our lives, and the fruit we bear, are still stamped with our own personalities, though—just as the rose scion still produces flashy flowers. But the source of our lives is Jesus, the rootstock. What's true of the rootstock becomes true of us. His life flows through us. It's pure, healthy, and strong.

Because we only see ourselves and not our rootstock, sometimes it's hard to believe we're grafted into Jesus. But it is true—and amazing! And it's important that we believe it. If we don't, we'll find ourselves struggling to live lives pleasing to God. Trying to live like Jesus in our own strength is like a branch trying to live apart from the vine. Can it? No—it shrivels up and dies! Just as the branch is dependent on the vine for life, we're dependent on Jesus to live His life through us.

Knowing that we're grafted into Jesus takes all the pressure off us to live for God. There's nothing hard about letting Jesus' life flow through us!

Jesus plus you equals one. Can you get any closer than that?

Thought to remember:
I'm grafted into Jesus.

Additional verses:
John 14:19b–20; 15:5b; 17:22–23; Genesis 3:22; 1 John 5:20

Let your imagination run wild. Could you graft tomato plants or roses onto an orange tree? No. Grafting only works between closely related plants. The more closely two plants are related, the more successful the graft will be.

TRY IT!

With your parents' permission, cut a small branch off a bush or tree. Lay the branch where you can observe it from time to time. How long does it take for the branch to dry out and become brittle? What color does the inside of the branch turn? If it has buds, do they open? If it has leaves, what happens to them? Does the branch bear fruit when it's separated from the tree?

DIG DEEPER!
★ plants
★ grafting

20 AMAZING ARMORED ANIMALS

This world can be a tough place to live!

To survive, plants and animals do many things to protect themselves. Wearing armor is one of them.

Armor can be something as simple as skin. Rhinos and elephants have extra thick hides to protect them from insects and enemies. Crocodiles and alligators wear tough scales. The **pangolin**—an anteater-like animal—has large scales that overlap like the scales of a pinecone. When a predator threatens, a pangolin curls into a ball to protect its tender underside.

Can you think of animals that use needles for prickly protection? Any animal that touches the point of a porcupine's quill is in for a surprise! And pain. Barbed tips make quills hard to remove.

Hedgehogs are prickly, too. Unlike the porcupine, though, hedgehogs don't lose their spines. For protection they tuck their stomach, feet, and face inside. It hurts to bite a ball of bristles!

Sea urchins are fist-sized ocean animals that are covered with long spikes to keep enemies away. Porcupine fish puff up like balloons to make their spines stick out. The trunks of giant **kapok** trees are covered with points. Roses are guarded by thorns. Spikes? Yikes! Keep away!

> FINALLY, LET THE LORD MAKE YOU STRONG. DEPEND ON HIS MIGHTY POWER. PUT ON ALL OF GOD'S ARMOR. THEN YOU CAN STAND FIRM AGAINST THE DEVIL'S EVIL PLANS.
>
> EPHESIANS 6:10–11

Many animals have outer bodies made of armor. Shells are hard homes that shelter the soft bodies of sea creatures. Crabs, shrimp, and lobsters wear stiff crusts that shape, support, and protect delicate insides. Insects have stiff crusts, too. Their skeletons are on the *outside*, not the inside as ours are. An outside skeleton is called an **exoskeleton**. Some exoskeletons come equipped with spikes and horns. Hard outer wing cases of ladybugs shield softer wings and body parts underneath.

The armadillo looks as if it is wearing a coat of armor—a better name might be *armor*-dillo. These strange creatures resemble short-legged pigs covered with a shell. This "shell" is made up of small bony plates with rough skin on top. The armor covers armadillos from their noses to the tips of their tails. The nine-banded armadillo has

---

pangolin:
(PAN-guh-lin)

The ladybug's hard outer wing case turns it into a tank. When attacked by ants, the ladybug simply lowers its shell to the ground. The curved, slick surface of its polka-dotted armor is impossible for ants to bite.

kapok:
(KAY-pock)

exoskeleton:
(ex-o-SKEL-eh-ten)

bony bands that protect its back and sides. Enemies can bite through this armor, though. An armadillo's main defense against predators is to run or burrow into the ground. Its armor allows it to escape and search for food in thorny plants and shrubs.

Humans wear armor, too. We wear helmets and an assortment of pads to protect our heads and bodies.

There's also another kind of armor we put on. God says that our battle isn't against people, but Satan. Satan wants us to disobey and doubt what God says. We don't have to fear him, though, because God defeated him. For our safety, God surrounds us with an unseen armor. God's powerful armor protects our hearts.

Our first piece of armor is a belt of truth. Jesus is the Truth. When we belong to Him, we're "wrapped" in Jesus, just as a belt wraps our bodies.

Our second piece of armor is the breastplate of righteousness. We've been made right with God because Jesus paid for our sins on the cross. This protects our hearts from guilt and fear.

Our feet also need boots to keep us from slipping in this world as we tell others about the peace Jesus gives us.

We hold the shield of faith in front of us. Believing what God says keeps us from believing the lies of Satan. The enemy's darts can't pierce a shield of faith.

We have confidence in Jesus' power to save us when we put on the helmet of salvation. He protects our heads, the source of our thoughts.

God also gives us a sword of the Spirit, God's Word. Knowing and believing what God says slices through Satan's lies.

Prayer adds the finishing shine to our armor. We can go straight to Him for anything we need.

This world can be a tough place to live, but God's armor makes us strong in His great power.

Thought to remember:
God's powerful armor protects me.

Additional verses:
Ephesians 6:10–18; Isaiah 52:7 (NIV); 59:17a; Zechariah 4:6 (NIV); Romans 8:31

The pink fairy armadillo has extra strange armor. Along with bands that protect its back, it has a flat bony plate that covers its rear end. When threatened, it burrows into the ground. The bony plate keeps out predators!

MATCH IT!

Below is a list of armor pieces that humans wear. Match the armor to the activity. In some cases, more than one answer is possible.

mouth guard	construction work
helmet	mountain biking
shin guard	hockey
wrist guard	wrestling
chest pad	soccer
knee pads	football
ear protection	police work
gloves	baseball
shoulder pads	fencing
bulletproof vest	inline skating
face mask	boxing
steel-toed boots	motorcycling

The answers are on page 152.

DIG DEEPER!

★ armored animals
★ skin
★ animal defenses
★ pangolin
★ insects
★ armadillo

21 WHO AM I?

The world inside a duck egg is warm and dark.

As the duckling pecks its way into the light, though, the time has come to begin a new life. Right away the duckling must learn how to stay safe and to find food. Who is the baby's teacher? Its mother.

But first the duckling must recognize who its mother is. This happens only in the first day of its life. During this time, the duckling sees and hears its mother. It follows and becomes attached to her. This process is called **imprinting**. Once a baby duck is imprinted on its mother, it doesn't confuse her with a rock or a stick. It can pick her out from the many other ducks around. The duckling will follow its mother while she feeds, swims, and stays out of danger. When ready, the baby will follow her into the sky.

imprinting:
(IM-prin-ting)

There are other baby animals who must imprint on their parents. Geese, goats, guinea pigs, sheep, zebras, and zebra **finches** are a few. All these young come into the world ready to eat and run within a few hours. For safety, they must quickly learn to follow their parents.

finch: a tiny bird, similar to a sparrow

Since the first few hours of these babies' lives are most important, is it possible for them to imprint on the wrong parent? A man who studied animal behavior, Konrad Lorenz, was the first to find out. He "adopted" newly hatched geese. The result? Picture a line of geese waddling after Lorenz, as they would their own mothers. These confused **goslings** attached to him and ignored other geese when they grew up. They thought they were people, not geese.

gosling:
(GOZ-ling)
a baby goose

People aren't the only substitute parents that animals have imprinted on. Buffalo have followed horses, zebras have bonded with cars. Some birds have been trained to follow moving boxes of a certain color.

On the other hand, geese that are kept completely alone for the first two days of their lives don't attach to anything. Once the imprinting time is over, it's too late.

> Brothers and sisters, we should always thank God for you. The Lord loves you. God chose you from the beginning. He wanted you to be saved. Salvation comes through the Holy Spirit's work. He makes people holy. It also comes through believing the truth.
>
> 2 THESSALONIANS 2:13

The lives of animals depend on knowing who they are and who their parents are. Did you know that this is important for you, too? "No, problem," you say. "I know who I am. I'm not a box or a car or a horse. *I* am a human being."

That's right. You are a human being.

But it's also important to know who God says you are. Sometimes instead of believing what God says, we believe things we hear from other people—things that aren't true. Then we're like geese who believe they're boxes when they're really geese.

Who does God say you are, once you've decided to follow Jesus? Listen to what He says:

* "You are no longer a slave to sin. Your sinful self died on the cross with my Son, Jesus. Now *my* life is in you" (see Romans 6:6, 8).

* "You are a saint, someone who is set apart for me" (see Ephesians 1:1, NIV).

* "I don't condemn you; don't condemn yourself" (see Romans 8:1, NIV).

* "You are very close to me." Jesus lives inside you and you live inside Him. You can't get any closer than that (see John 14:20).

* "You are important enough to know me, the Creator of the universe" (see Jeremiah 9:24).

* "You are special. I love you dearly. I delight in you" (see Zephaniah 3:17).

It's never too late to start believing what God says about you. You, too, can imprint on your Father, God. Your life will be filled with peace, rest, and joy.

Thought to remember:
Who does God say that I am? That's what counts.

Additional verses:
Romans 6:6–8; Philippians 1:1 (NIV); John 14:20; 17:3; Colossians 3:12

EXPLORE IT!

Get ready to play The Imprinting Game, for two to three players. For this game, you need twenty-three index cards. Write the names of each of the following animals on a *separate* card:

gosling	mother goose
duckling	mother duck
zebra foal	mother zebra
foal	mother horse
buffalo calf	mother buffalo
chick	mother hen
gull chick	mother gull
lamb	mother sheep
kid	mother goat
California condor chick	mother California condor
ostrich chick	father ostrich
	imprinted on a person

The object of this game is to get rid of all your cards first. Mix the cards. Deal five cards to each person. Set the extra cards on the table, face side down. Take turns picking a card from the other player(s) or from the pile. When you match the baby with the right parent, you can set the pair aside. Try not to be left holding the "imprinted on a person" card!

DIG DEEPER!

* animal behavior
* imprinting
* baby animals

Do you ever dream that you can fly? With your arms stretched wide, you lift into the sky. How free it feels to sail over the earth with the birds!

But as soon as the dream ends, your feet are back on the ground. What is it about birds that makes them able to fly? There are several pieces to this puzzle:

* Bird bones are light. They're not solid like ours, but hollow. And yet they're strong—a web of fine bones inside gives extra support.

* Another puzzle piece is a bird's skull. It doesn't have heavy teeth in a large jaw to weigh it down. Instead, it has a toothless bill that is hollow yet strong.

* A bird skeleton is built in a way that helps it hold up under the pressures of flight. Some bones, such as the ribs, are joined together for strength. Joints move in unusual ways to allow these feathered animals to cruise through the sky. The extraordinarily big breastbone connects to huge flight muscles.

> FOR GOD DID NOT give us a SPIRIT of timidity, but a SPIRIT of Power, of Love and of Self-DiscipLine.
>
> 2 TIMOTHY 1:7
> (NIV)

* A big piece of the puzzle is feathers. You've heard the phrase "light as a feather." Even though bird feathers weigh next to nothing, they're strong. In the center of the feather is the long shaft. Hundreds of fine strands, called barbs, fan out from both sides of the shaft. They make up the colored part of the feather. Many shorter strands, called **barbules,** branch out of each barb. Tiny hooks on the barbules grab onto the barbules across from them, holding the feather together as it slices through air.

  Most of the bird's body is covered with **contour** feathers. These give the bird a smooth shape so it can glide easily. Tail and wing feathers are light but stiff.

* Do birds fly by flapping their wings? That's just part of it. The curved shape of the wing is another puzzle piece. As air moves past the wing, it has to move faster over the top of the curve. This makes the air pressure lower on top than on the bottom. The greater pressure on the bottom

barbule:
(BARB-you'll)

contour:
(CON-tour)

causes the wing to lift. Then, as the bird flaps its wings, the outer wing feathers twist and separate to act as propellers. This is how a bird rises and moves forward through the air.

★ To top it off, birds have special lungs to supply muscles with the extra oxygen needed to fly.

When you put all these puzzle pieces together, you can understand why birds can fly. Birds are born to fly.

And in a way, so are we. We "fly" when we love others. We are born to love.

What is it about us that makes us able to love? It's simply Jesus living inside us. That's because Jesus is God, and God is love.

This is how He loves:

God is

always patient,

always kind.

He is

never jealous of others,

never proud, rude, or self-centered.

God is

not easily angered.

And He

doesn't brag about himself.

But He

always forgives, always forgets.

He

always protects, trusts, and always hopes.

God

never gives up on us.

(s e e 1 C O R I N T H I A N S 1 3)

This is how God wants us to love others. But if you've ever tried to love like this, you know it's like trying to fly without wings.

With Jesus' life inside us, though, the puzzle is complete. When we give up trying to do it ourselves and ask God to love through us, loving is as natural as flying. Jesus shows His love for others through us. Then we can love our families and friends and people we don't know—even people we don't *like*.

Each day God puts people in our lives to love. When we do, we soar above jealousy, hate, and selfishness. We fly, free as a bird.

The penguin "flies" through water. Its wings act as paddles, and its feet are used to steer. Tiny feathers cover a penguin's body to help it glide through water.

Terns are gull-like birds. They have long, pointed wings and forked tails that make it possible for them to stay in the air a long, long time. Sooty terns spend months gliding over the ocean—without landing. Scientists believe they even sleep in the air.

THINK ABOUT IT!

Find a quiet corner to think about God's love.

When God handed Jesus over to hateful men to be killed, He handed over someone He dearly loved—His Son. How could He do that?

It meant everything to God for us to be able to have a close relationship with Him. His love for us is amazing—more than we can take in.

TRY IT!

See for yourself how lift on a bird's wing takes place. Hold one end of a sheet of paper between both hands in front of your face. Let the far end of the paper curve down. Now blow over the top surface of the paper. The far end will rise as long as you blow on the paper. This shows how differences in air pressure cause lift.

DIG DEEPER!

* how birds fly
* animal flight
* birds

Thought to remember:

Jesus' life in me makes me able to love others as He loves.

Additional verses:

1 John 4:10–12; John 14:20; 15:5, 12–13; 1 Corinthians 16:14

23

Beasts of Burden

How strong are you?

Can you lift ten pounds? Twenty-five? Perhaps you're a body builder who can lift fifty.

Humans can carry large loads compared to their size. But often we need help. Today we turn to tractors, trucks, and other machines to help us move our goods. But in the past, beasts of **burden** have pushed, pulled, lifted, and carried our cargo. Some still do.

The "truck of the **Andes**," or **llama**, is one of these. For centuries this member of the camel family has helped humans in the mountains of Peru and Bolivia. In the past few years, the llama has become a popular pack animal in North America, too. Perhaps you've seen this furry deer-shaped creature with long neck and legs.

A four-hundred-pound llama is able to pack about one hundred pounds on its back. Llamas can't pack as much as a donkey or a horse, but there are advantages to using them. They don't cost much to feed. These calm creatures are easily taught to follow in a pack train. The two fleshy pads that form their feet allow them to travel safely on rocky and slippery trails, and they don't damage trails.

Another beast of burden is the mule. This long-eared animal is a mix between a male horse and female donkey. A mule that weighs about one thousand pounds can carry over two hundred pounds. That's twice as much as a llama can carry.

Compared to horses, mules are tougher and more sure-footed. Perhaps you've heard the phrase "stubborn as a mule." Those who work with mules claim they aren't stubborn—but they do take a bit more patience to train. Perhaps a better phrase might be "cool as a mule." because they're less likely to panic in dangerous situations.

Mules are great beasts of burden. But compared with elephants, they're shrimps. As the largest land animals, elephants are the Samsons of the animal world. Male African elephants weigh about 12,000 pounds. Even the slightly smaller male Asian

> "Come to me, all of you who are tired and are carrying heavy loads. I will give you rest. Become my servants and learn from me. I am gentle and free of pride. You will find rest for your souls. Serving me is easy, and my load is light."
>
> MATTHEW 11:28–30

Camels are still used today to bear our burdens. The word *camel* comes from a word that means "carrying a burden." These ships of the desert carry and pull heavy loads. Depending on their size, camels can move five hundred to one thousand pounds on their backs.

TRY IT!

Load a backpack with enough weight to make it feel heavy to you. Carry it in your arms or on your back for as long as you can. When you finally get rid of your burden, how do you feel? Are your tired muscles glad? Do you feel light?

The heavy loads we carry in our hearts may not be felt in our arms or legs. But when we let God take over our struggles and problems, we feel glad and our steps are lighter.

DIG DEEPER!

* llama
* elephant
* mule
* camel

elephants are a hefty 10,000. They can pull about half their weight—or carry about 1,200 pounds on their backs.

Not only do these king-sized animals carry mammoth burdens, but they drag and lift, as well. In Thailand and India, loggers use elephants to lift logs and push or pull them to rivers. They carry tourists into national parks. Elephants can go where machines can't.

Animals help us by bearing our burdens. Jesus does, too. He carries the burdens of our hearts—problems and struggles that make us feel worried or afraid. We're not meant to carry them. They make us tired. Sometimes we feel like giving up. That's why He said, "Come to me, all of you who are tired and are carrying heavy loads."

The reason Jesus came to earth in the first place is because God knew we needed help. Sin is a heavy burden. When Jesus died on the cross, He took the weight of our sins on himself. Jesus wants us to trade our heavy load of sin for his light load. He wants us to give Him the control of our lives. Then we find rest.

Jesus also carries the weight of our everyday problems, even when we think it would take an elephant to carry them. As we get to know Him, we find out how much Jesus loves us. We learn how gentle and patient He is. Then we understand that we can trust Him with the burdens of our lives and gladly turn them over to Him. Turning our problems over to Jesus takes away fear and worry and gives us relief.

Is something troubling you? Go to Jesus and learn from Him. Give Him your life and all your problems. You can trust Him to take care of you.

How many fifty-pound kids could ride on an elephant? About twenty-four!

Thought to remember:
Jesus carries all my burdens.

Additional verses:
Psalm 28:9 (NIV); 38:4; Isaiah 53:4, 6; Philippians 4:6–7

24

THERE'S NO PLACE LIKE HOME

Imagine your favorite place to live.

Are you sitting in a castle, a condo, a tree house, or a mobile home? Is it built of concrete, wood, bricks, or even sticks? Did you put in heating and air conditioning? A swimming pool?

Let's tour homes in the world of animals to see how they live. We'll begin with a castle—a sand castle.

The soldier crab builds a sand castle on the beach for protection from drowning in the rising tide. This crab digs a shallow pit with its claws, then pushes up pellets of sand into a mud dome. By plugging the hole in the ceiling, this animal **architect** seals a bubble of air in and the water out.

Our next stop is a pond. If you watch carefully you might see twigs or a pile of pebbles scoot along the bottom. No, they're not alive. You are watching the original mobile home, the home of a **caddis fly larva**. These caterpillars have soft bodies that need protection. When they hatch, they spin a silk tube around their bodies. To strengthen the tube, they add pebbles, shells, twigs, and leaves. Any time this caterpillar is frightened, it pulls its head and front legs into its home.

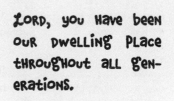

LORD, you Have been OUR DWELLING PLace throughout aLL generations.

PSALM 90:1 (NIV)

While we're at the pond, let's check out underwater tents. The water spider has no gills, yet it lives underwater. How? First this spider spins a silk tent between plants. Swimming to the surface, it traps an air bubble between its **abdomen** and hind legs. Diving back to its silk tent, the spider frees the bubble. After several trips, the tent bulges with air.

The spider's most important needs are met inside this home. Like a scuba diver, the water spider always carries an air supply—tiny air bubbles trapped on body hairs. But when that supply runs out, the spider returns to the tent for more. This oxygen tent is also home base for hunting. And inside the bubble, it mates and stores its eggs.

Back on land we'll catch our breath and visit an **adobe** home. The female potter wasp builds a pot to care for her young. First she finds clay soil. If the clay is too dry, she softens it with water from her stomach. Scooping small balls with her mouthparts

Margin glossary

architect: (AR-kih-tekt) someone who designs buildings

caddis fly larva: (KA-dus fly ZAR-vuh)

abdomen: (AB-doe-men) the third or last section on the body of an insect

adobe: (uh-DOE-bee) a clay used to make bricks

Some animal homes have air conditioning. Termites are antlike creatures that live in mounds. Several types of termite mounds have air ducts that let fresh air in and stale air out. Some termites use chimneys to bring in fresh air.

TRY IT!

See for yourself how the water spider traps air underwater. Fill a sink with water and color it with your favorite color of food coloring. Hold a clear glass upside down and press it under the water. You'll see trapped air at the top of the glass, above the colored water. This is similar to the air trapped under the silk tent that the water spider uses as an underwater nest.

MATCH IT!

Match the animal's home with the picture it gives of God.

God is always with you	
God protects you	potter wasp nest
God cares for you, His child	water spider
	caddis fly larva
God takes care of your most important needs	soldier crab

The answers are on page 152.

DIG DEEPER!

★ animal architects
★ animal builders
★ animal homes

and front legs, she carries them to her construction site. Here she shapes a fat little pot with a narrow neck. The mother stocks the pot with paralyzed caterpillars, lays an egg inside, and plugs the opening. As soon as the wasp larva hatches, it's ready to eat this jarful of baby food.

Animals live in all kinds of homes, don't they? No matter how simple or fancy, there's no place like home to find shelter from enemies and the weather, to raise young, to catch and store food.

People use homes for shelter and safety, to raise children, and store food, too. But a home is more than wood, brick, and glass—more than a place where you're fed and clothed and sheltered from storms. A home is a place where you belong and feel loved.

God gives us families to care for us in our homes. But no matter how much your family loves you, there are times when you can still feel lonely or hurt inside. The people closest to you can let you down.

That's why God calls himself your home. Not only does He take care of the needs of your body, He wants to take care of the loneliness and hurts you have inside, too. Like the castle of the soldier crab, He seals you inside the bubble of His love. Like the shell of the caddis fly larva, He's always with you. You can hide inside Him when you're afraid. Like the tent of the water spider and the pot of the potter wasp larva, He takes care of all of your needs, both inside and out. There's no one who cares for you as much as God does. He is your refuge.

Thought to remember:
There's no home like God.

Additional verses:
Psalm 62:8; 5:11; 91:4, 9; Acts 17:28; Philippians 4:19

25 Migration Marathons

You've probably heard of marathons—twenty-six-mile races that test the strength and endurance of human runners. Did you know that billions and billions of animals take part in marathons every year? The strength of all kinds of animals is tested as they fly, swim, walk, hop, and slither to winter homes and back again. These marathons are called migrations.

migration:
(my-GRAY-shun)
the movement of
animals from
one place to
another and
back again

Most migrations are greater than twenty-six miles. Birds called arctic terns win the gold medal for the longest journey. They feed and raise their young in Arctic areas where the sun never sets in the summer. In late summer, these black-capped birds leave the top of the world. About three months later they arrive at the bottom of the world, in Antarctica. Here they feed on treasures of small fish during long days without nights. When Antarctic days begin to shorten, the tern's return trip north to the Arctic begins. By migrating up to 25,000 miles a year, terns enjoy the best of both worlds—constant sunlight.

Black-poll warblers win a prize for nonstop flights from the east coast of North America to South America. Before leaving on a nonstop, three- to four-day marathon across the Atlantic Ocean, these tiny birds become little "fatties" by doubling their weight. A 2,500-mile trip to South America requires a lot of energy, and there are no restaurants along the way!

The top award for the most amazing migration goes to monarch butterflies. In early fall, clouds of monarchs flutter south from Canada and the United States. Some spend the winter in southern California. The rest fly up to three thousand miles to reach mountains in the middle of Mexico.

Tree trunks and branches turn orange where these tiger-striped butterflies cluster. Although monarchs are light as leaves, large numbers of butterflies make branches sag and sometimes break.

> Don't you know who made everything? Haven't you heard about Him? The Lord is the God who lives forever. He created everything on earth. He won't become worn out or get tired. No one will ever know how great His understanding is. He gives strength to those who are tired. He gives power to those who are weak.
>
> ISAIAH 40:28-29

Bar-headed geese win first place for high-altitude migrations. They fly over the **Himalaya** (Him-uh-LAY-uh) Mountains, reaching heights up to 29,500 feet.

The blue grouse comes in last place for migration feats. These chickenlike birds *walk* about one thousand feet up mountain slopes for wintertime.

TRY IT!

Every year, animals are tagged to track their migrations. You and your family or classmates can try it this fall. To order instructions and tags for monarch butterflies, contact one of the following organizations:

If you live east of the Rocky Mountains:

> Monarch Watch
> 1-888-TAGGING
> www.monarchwatch.org

If you live west of the Rocky Mountains:

> David Marriott
> The Monarch Program
> P.O. Box 178671
> San Diego, CA 92177
> 1-760-944-7113
> monarchprg@aol.com

DIG DEEPER!

* animal migration
* migration
* monarch butterflies
* birds

During the second week of March, monarch butterflies begin another flight north on tattered wings. Mating and feeding along the way, females lay eggs as soon as they find milkweed. But out of energy, most of these monarchs won't make it to their birthplace. Their caterpillars develop into adult butterflies, finishing the journey north.

Although most animals migrate safely every year, dangers along the way take many lives. Migrating animals become food for predators. Bad weather catches them by surprise. Some might also run out of energy. But many animals whose homes turn icy and whose food disappears in winter have no choice but to migrate.

Sometimes we might feel like we're in migration marathons. When we're expected to do more than we think we can, our strength is tested—just like a migrating animal. Perhaps school seems too hard, our families have problems, or we struggle with friendships. At times we grow tired of trying and just feel like giving up.

Birds prepare for migration by putting on fat. Important flight muscles become bigger than ever. A new set of flight feathers replaces old ones. We can be ready for challenges in our lives, too. How?

By resting in Jesus, the One who never grows tired or weary. When He lives inside us, He becomes our strength—our spiritual energy, muscles, and feathers. With His power, we can travel through the marathons of life and "run" without growing tired. With His power we don't have to worry about whether we can make it or not.

What Jesus can do is far greater than anything man can do. His *weakness* is much stronger than the strength of man. We can count on Jesus' strength in any situation. He is our strength.

Thought to remember:

God is my strength.

Additional verses:

Isaiah 40:30–31; Philippians 4:13; 1 Corinthians 1:25; Psalm 73:26; 105:4; Habakkuk 3:19; Ephesians 6:10

If you decided to go on a long trip, would you hop into the car and just start driving?

Probably not! You would get out a map and trace the best route to get where you're going.

When animals migrate, they don't use road maps. They don't follow roads. They don't stop and ask for directions. So how do they get where they want to go without getting lost?

navigate:
(NAV-ih-gate)

One way animals find their way, or **navigate**, is by checking the position of the sun. Homing pigeons use the sun as a compass to show the way.

What about birds that fly at night? As you might guess, they follow the stars. The indigo bunting, a sparrowlike bird, uses constellations surrounding the North Star.

But what happens when clouds hide the sun or stars?

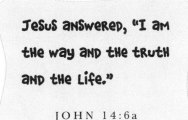
Jesus answered, "I am the way and the truth and the life."

JOHN 14:6a

magnetic:
(mag-NET-ik)acts Like a magnet

Scientists think that pigeons and other birds sense direction by using a force that surrounds the earth. You've probably played with magnets before. The earth has a **magnetic** force around it that pigeons can use as a guide.

Scientists believe night flyers may also use sounds such as waves crashing on faraway beaches. They may follow special smells that give them clues about their location.

salmon:
(SAM-en)
a Large fish

fry: a young,
newly hatched
fish

One fish that sniffs its way home is the **salmon**. After hatching, these small **fry** swim down rivers and streams and out to the ocean. Several years later adult salmon use familiar smells to guide their return upstream—to the exact river where they were born. There they lay their eggs.

Some young birds follow family members to learn migration routes. This is the case for swans. They form mental maps of mountains, fields, and rivers, remembering them from year to year and passing them from generation to generation.

But some creatures, such as monarch butterflies, don't have parents to lead them to winter homes. How do they know where to fly in the fall? Were they born with an understanding of the direction they must take? Probably. No one really knows.

Scientists use different tools to solve the mysteries of animal navigation.

* The most common tool is a tag. Birds are caught in delicate nets. Scientists fit small bands, like bracelets, to the birds' legs. Then the birds are freed. When people find a banded bird, they send the date and location to the address on the band.
* Radio transmitters are attached to animals, as well. These send out signals that can be followed with receivers.
* Scientists also track birds on **radar** (RAY-dar), an instrument used to locate airplanes. Radar can show how fast a flock of birds is flying, its size, and its direction.
* Another method is to follow animals using aircraft.

TRY IT!

Test your own sense of direction. Go outside with your parents. Have them show you where north, south, east, and west are. Then let them blindfold you. After they lead you about and turn you in circles, can you still point to the south? You might be surprised at your sense of direction! Try this experiment on other family members.

DIG DEEPER!

* animal navigation
* animal migration

Many mysteries still cloud our understanding of animal navigation. But whether we understand or not, it's clear that several systems are at work inside animals to direct them on the paths they must follow.

In a way, we're like migrating animals. We're all on a trip without maps. That trip is our lives, and sometimes we feel lost. We grope and try to find our own way. Without a map, sometimes it's pretty hard to know which way to go.

What we need is a way to navigate.

Birds check the sun; we check with the *Son*—Jesus. He's our compass, pointing our way to a relationship with God. After that He continues to be our direction as we travel through life. He has a plan for each of our lives, so we don't have to worry about figuring it out for ourselves. Living inside us, He guides our decisions—what we do and how we live.

From time to time, migrating birds are blown off course, but the inner workings that guide them remain inside. When storms rage in our lives and we feel lost, we can take comfort knowing that Jesus remains inside, guiding us. He's our steady compass. As we travel step by step counting on Jesus, He'll direct our journeys through life.

Thought to remember:

Jesus is my compass.

Additional verses:

Proverbs 3:5–6; Psalm 43:3; 139:9–10; Isaiah 42:16; John 16:13

To discover more about monarch butterfly migrations, turn to "Migration Marathons" on page 65.

27 GLOW-in-the-DARK FiSH

bioLumineScence:
(by-OH-LOOM-in-ES-ense)

WHat aRe tHe
coLoRS of tHe
Rainbow?
Red, ORange,
YeLLow, GReen,
BLue, Indigo, and
VioLet. HeRe'S an
easy way to
RememBeR tHem:
Put togetHeR tHe
fiRSt LetteR of
eacH coLoR to
SPeLL tHe name
ROY G. BIV.

WHat do bacteRia
tHat gLow in tHe
daRK Receive in
excHange foR
HeLPing tHe fiSH
tHey Live witH?
Food and oxygen.
To diScoveR moRe
aBout animaLS
tHat HeLP eacH
otHeR, tuRn to
"PoSitive
PaRtneRSHiPS" on
Page 115.

Imagine you're in a submarine, diving into the ocean.

Deeper and deeper you descend; the water turns to dusk, then night. By three thousand feet there's hardly a trace of light. Four thousand feet, five thousand feet. When you cut your headlights, it's so dark you can't even see your hand in front of you.

But after a while lights twinkle out of the darkness. Have the stars fallen to the bottom of the ocean? No, these "stars" are alive. Down here, where there is no light, all kinds of sea creatures make their own.

You flip your headlights on again. An ugly angler fish with sharp teeth is staring at you. It has a "fishing rod" made of flesh that rises from its nose. A lighted "lure" dangles from the end of the rod. The angler fish gobbles up fish that are attracted to this light. *Chomp. Gulp.* How's that for home delivery?

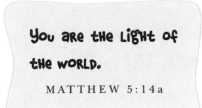

You are the Light of the world.

MATTHEW 5:14a

Bioluminescence is the word used for light given off by living things. Light is made when two chemicals mix with oxygen. Spots of light are arranged in many patterns on the bodies of these deep-sea animals. These lights come in the colors of the rainbow, plus pink and white. Some marine animals actually carry bacteria that produce the chemicals for them.

That's the case with the lantern, or flashlight, fish. These fish have half-moon-shaped pouches under each eye. Each pouch carries bacteria that shine like a flashlight to help the lantern fish find food. Some fish can even turn off their lights by raising their lower lids to cover the pouches!

Creatures use living lights to help them find food. But shining lights also keep some fish from becoming food. Custom lights might signal to hunters that their prey won't taste good. One type of worm sheds glowing scales when it's in danger. The predator is distracted by the flashing scales while the worm makes its getaway. Other fish and squid shoot out bright ink screens that confuse the enemy.

In a dark undersea world, some creatures also use living lights to find each other. It's a way for mates to say, "Here I am." Pairs of fish may also blink their lights in special patterns to communicate with each other or to defend territories.

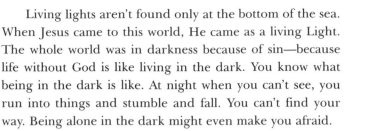

In some species of angler fish, only the female has lures. The male, who is much smaller, attaches to a female. He exists as a parasite hooked to his mate. Once attached, the male's body shrinks; his blood vessels connect to the blood vessels of the female he's joined with.

Bioluminescent animals also live on land. You may have seen fireflies blinking on warm summer evenings. A glowworm that lives in New Zealand caves creates silken threads that hang from the ceiling. Sticky droplets on the threads glow to attract small flies for dinner. Some species of millipedes, earthworms, snails, mold, and bacteria also glow in the dark.

MAKE IT!

See for yourself how living lights shine out of darkness. You will need a foot-long piece of foil, a pin or needle, and a flashlight.

Poke holes in the foil with the pin. You may need to lift one corner of the foil to do this. You can poke holes in any design, such as the shape of a fish or your initials.

Then take your foil and flashlight into a room without windows. Turn off the light. Press the flashlight against the back of the foil to see the pattern that the light casts onto the wall. Can you see how a living light shines out of the darkness?

DIG DEEPER!

* bioluminescence
* living lights
* animals, glow

Living lights aren't found only at the bottom of the sea. When Jesus came to this world, He came as a living Light. The whole world was in darkness because of sin—because life without God is like living in the dark. You know what being in the dark is like. At night when you can't see, you run into things and stumble and fall. You can't find your way. Being alone in the dark might even make you afraid.

But Jesus is a bright Light shining out of the darkness. He is the Light of the World so that people can find their way back to God and have light by which to live their daily lives. His light draws many people to God.

When you believe that Jesus died for your sins and you choose to follow Him, He comes to live inside you. He chases out the darkness and becomes the Light of your life. Then His light shines out of you. He makes you a living light that shines out of the darkness, too. You become a light for people to find their way to God.

Thought to remember:

Jesus is the living Light. He makes me one, too.

Additional verses:

John 8:12; 2 Corinthians 4:6; Psalm 18:28; Ephesians 5:8–9

28 To Spin a Web

§piders all over the world spin webs. They make themselves at home everywhere—in castles and cabins, fields and forests, banks and barns. Some build broad sheets and hammocks of silk on bushes. Others build funnels. Black widows build platforms of uneven strands that look as if there's no pattern to them at all. The most familiar web is one you'd recognize—that of the orb web spider. It weaves a wheel-shaped web on a frame of spokes.

HAMMOCK: (HAM-uck) a bed that hangs between two supports

Now, picture this. You're streaking through the woods on your bike. It's a sunny day; sunlight flickers through the trees. The trail curves and dips. Imagine your surprise when your face rips through a tangle of sticky threads.

Imagine the spider's surprise, too. You just shattered its trap. How will it rebuild the web?

Let's watch. . . .

First the orb web spider lets out a strand of silk that sails through the air. If the strand catches on a branch or wire, it forms a bridge. The spider reinforces it with more silk lines, then drops from the middle of the bridge to pull it into a Y shape. From this skeleton, the spider strings a frame and adds spokes that join at the center—like the spokes of your bicycle. Beginning at the center and working its way out, the spider then lays down a spiral of dry, non-sticky silk. When it reaches the outside, the spider turns around and lays a tighter spiral of sticky threads, eating the dry spiral as it works. It's on these gluey strands that insects will be trapped. Now the web is complete. Crawling to a platform at the center or to a shelter at the side, the spider holds on to a thread of the trap and waits, like a fisherman holding his fishing pole.

How does a spider avoid being trapped in its own web? It steps along its web with special claws. An oil on its legs keeps it from sticking if it happens to touch a sticky thread.

DON'T LIE to each other. You have gotten rid of your old way of Life and its habits. You have started Living a new Life. It is being made new so that what you know has the Creator's Likeness.

COLOSSIANS 3:9–10

vibration: (vy-BRAY-shun) quick back-and-forth movements

What happens when an insect crashes into this net? The spider feels the **vibrations** of the struggling insect. By touching different spokes, the spider can tell the exact location of its victim. After a paralyzing bite, the spider wraps its prey in a cocoon of silk and carries the victim to its shelter to be eaten.

Where does a spider's silk come from? Inside a spider are several organs that produce different types of silk for different jobs. These organs are hooked to tubes that run to **spinnarets** (spin-uh-RETS) at the rear of the spider. Spider silk starts out as a liquid but hardens into a thread as it leaves the spinnaret and meets the air.

FIND IT!

For this activity, you need hair spray, a pair of scissors, and a piece of black construction paper. Search for a wheel-shaped orb web among plants and tree branches or along a fence. When you find one—and if there is no spider in the center—spray it lightly with hair spray several times. Place the black paper behind it and snip off the strands of silk that attach it to supports. Spray it again so it will stick to the paper. Find the hub at the center, where the spider waits. Can you see areas where trapped insects have ripped the web?

DIG DEEPER!

* spiders
* spider webs

Spiders spin webs of silk to catch dinner. Sometimes we spin webs of lies. Who gets caught in our webs?

We do.

Perhaps you've heard or read this saying:

Oh what a tangled web we weave,
*When first we practise to **deceive**!*

—SIR WALTER SCOTT

The spider spins a bridge, a frame, and spokes, then the sticky spiral. When we tell one lie, we have to spin another to cover up the first one. More lies follow. Before we know it, we've woven the bridge, frame, spokes, and sticky spiral.

And just as insects are snared in webs, we're caught in our own web of lies. How? After a while, we lose track of what the truth is. We can't possibly remember all the lies we've told to cover up other lies. Sometimes we even begin to believe them ourselves. Then people can't trust us anymore. They see that we're not honest.

The worst part is that when we tell lies to others, we aren't honest with God, either. A person might not be able to tell we're lying, but we can't hide anything from God. He knows everything about us.

What if you're caught in this trap? Tell the Father what you've done. Remember that God is Truth—He loves for us to be honest with Him. He's ready to forgive.

Next, ask for forgiveness from those you've lied to. Be ready to accept the **consequences** of your lies.

Then refuse to tell even one more lie. Tell the truth instead. Being honest frees you from the tangled web of deceit. It frees your heart from the torment of guilt. The truth will set you free.

Thought to remember:

Lying is a trap.

Additional verses:

John 3:21; Psalm 51:6; Proverbs 19:5; 24:26; 26:28a

deceive: (DIH-SEEVE) to cause someone to believe something that isn't true

consequence: (CON-sih-kwents) the result that follows an action

29 Recipe for Life

Let's try out a new recipe.

It's not a recipe for food. This is a pretend recipe for something that grows food: soil.

Let's begin with tiny bits of clay and sand. These come from rocks that are worn down by wind and water. Sprinkle on a layer of dead plants, leaves, and animals. This layer is called litter. Now blend in a big scoop of **microscopic** creatures—bacteria and **fungi**. To this add all kinds of tiny animals—living animals such as ants, beetles, spiders, snails, millipedes, and roly-polies. Include large ones such as skunks, mice, and birds, too.

What happens in our soil stew?

All the living critters hunt for food. They eat each other. Some of them also eat the dead plants and animals. The breakdown of these plant and animal bodies is called **decay**. Bacteria and fungi are especially good at making things decay. In this way plants and animals are recycled. Other plants and animals can use the nutrients stored in their bodies.

Over time, the litter becomes black and crumbly. It's now **humus**, an important building block for rich dirt. As humus mixes with the tiny bits of rock, it looks and feels like soil. It becomes topsoil, the layer of earth where plants grow. Seeds fall on it. If we sprinkle on some rain, these sprout. Plant roots spread throughout the topsoil. Stems and leaves grow upward to catch food from the sun. They become the source of food for all animals.

While the plants grow, throw in a batch of earthworms. They plow through the dark dirt, eating it. What isn't digested comes out as waste, or castings. Moving the soil about in this way keeps it loose and gives it air spaces. The soil breathes. Water soaks in. This makes the soil healthy for all living things that grow there.

Other animals that like moist, dark homes—moles, roundworms, mites, and various insects—also live in the topsoil.

Now our soil is a web of plants and animals that depend on one another. It's alive.

microscopic: (my-cro-SCOP-ik) things that can be seen only with a microscope

fungi: (FUN-jeye) plural for fungus (FUN-gus). A group of living things, similar to plants, that don't have leaves, flowers, or green coloring. Mushrooms and molds are fungi.

decay: (Dee-KAY)

humus: (HYU-mus)

> Then he said to all of them, "If anyone wants to follow me, he must say no to himself. He must pick up his cross every day and follow me. If he wants to save his life, he will lose it. But if he loses his life for me, he will save it."
>
> LUKE 9:23–24

Why do earthworms rush above ground when it rains? Water floods their burrows, and they begin to drown. Once they are above ground, though, they dry out. Unless they burrow into the topsoil again, they become bird food.

The first mold used as an antibiotic lives in the soil. A man named Alexander Fleming discovered it. He noticed that bacteria didn't grow near the mold. Fleming learned that the mold puts out a poison that kills bacteria. This poison was developed into the antibiotic penicillin, which kills harmful bacteria in your body.

EXPLORE IT!

Mark off one square foot in the soil. Dig out three to four inches of the soil and spread it out over newspaper. Make a list of each life-form you find. How many of each type are there? Describe how each type of animal moves. If you have a magnifying glass, use it to discover even smaller animals.

DIG DEEPER!

* soil
* how soil is made
* the living earth

Over and over the process is repeated. Creatures live, eat, and have young. They leave behind droppings that other animals eat. They die, and their bodies are recycled so that other creatures—including you—can live and grow. The recipe for soil is really a recipe for life that comes out of death.

Here's another recipe for life.

Jesus said that if we want to follow Him, we must pick up our crosses every day. A cross is a place of death. Why would Jesus say that?

He showed us by His life.

In order to walk on this earth as a man, Jesus suffered great losses to himself. To become a man, He didn't hold on to who He was as God, but made himself as if He were nothing. In the end He even lost His life. Why? To give us life.

God knew that our sinful selves, which are disobedient to Him, couldn't be fixed up or changed. Instead, they had to be done away with. When Jesus died on the cross, He took our sinful selves to the cross, and we died along with Him. Then when Jesus rose from the dead, we also rose with Him. By choosing death for himself, Jesus made it possible for us to have new life in our spirits. When we believe in Jesus, He lives inside us and loves through us.

Sometimes, though, we still want to depend on ourselves, especially in tough situations. But holding on tight to our own way of doing things doesn't work very well. That's where the cross comes in. As we depend on Jesus to work things out, we experience a sort of death to our own way of doing things. Then His life can be expressed through us and touch the lives of others.

Soil is made up of the lives of plants and animals that have died. Their death makes soil rich and bursting with life. Turning to God may bring death to our own way, but it also makes us burst forth with life—God's life.

Thought to remember:
Jesus is a source of life to others through me.

Additional verses:
Matthew 10:38–39; Philippians 2:3–8; John 12:24–26; 15:12–13; 2 Corinthians 4:10–12 (NIV)

Vs blast, radios drum. Dryers buzz, computers hum.
Dogs bark, sirens scream. Jets roar, telephones ring.
Our world is full of noise!

There's another sound we hear every day, though many of us might not notice. It's a sound behind the clutter of noise in our lives. It's the sound of singing—the songs of birds.

Humans enjoy the trills, whistles, and warbles of birds. But did you know that birdsongs have a purpose?

Just as humans talk to each other, singing is a way for birds to communicate. Songs can ripple through air over long distances, day and night. Birds living in thick forests or bushes use sounds to keep track of each other.

> Sing and make music in your heart to the Lord.
>
> EPHESIANS 5:19b

A bird's song is like Caller ID. Through their tunes, one species of bird tells another who they are. Some species look so much alike, their songs may be the only way to tell each other apart.

To discover more about how animals communicate, turn to "In a World Without Words" on page 79.

Just as we can tell each other apart by differences in our voices, individual birds also recognize each other by slight differences in *song*. This is important for feathered parents and their babies, who need to find each other in the midst of thousands of nests. The same is true for mates. Imagine what could happen if a male landed at the wrong nest. Birds also need to know who their neighbors are; personal songs are one way to do that.

Many bird sounds are short and simple. These are alarm calls to warn other birds to hide because a predator is near. Loud cries may also signal birds to come together to mob a hawk or squirrel. Chirps, honks, peeps, quacks, and caws are only a few of the sounds that bring birds together to flock, nest, and eat.

Longer songs—those like the melodies in our own music—are used by males to warn other males to stay out of their territories. These more complicated songs are also ways of inviting females to join them. By singing, males advertise their species, age, and location.

Birds may also call and sing just for the joy of it. We may never know if this is true

Most birds know five to fourteen calls and songs. Some, like parrots, skylarks, and mockingbirds, invent new songs by copying other birds. Others, such as mute swans and turkey vultures, only grunt or hiss now and then.

One type of African bush shrike sings **duets** (dew-ETS). Duets are sung by mates to keep track of each other and to protect their territory. They sing so closely together that it's hard to tell that two birds, not one, are singing.

CHECK IT OUT!

Borrow a CD of birdsongs from your local library. Do you recognize any of the songs of birds that live in your neighborhood? Go on a walk to discover birdsongs you've never noticed before.

DIG DEEPER!

* animal behavior
* songbirds
* birdsong

or not, but it's something we can relate to—we often sing because we enjoy it, too.

That is especially true when we sing to the Lord. He puts a new song in our hearts at the beginning of our relationship with Him. Because God loves us, we sing. And because we love God, we sing to Him. It's a way of praising and worshiping the Lord. It's a way of saying thanks for all He does for us. It's a way of telling Him how amazed we are that He is in our lives.

Just as male birds sing to announce themselves to the world, singing is our way of announcing to the whole world that we're glad we belong to God. Singing about all God's works encourages our hearts and comforts us during hard times. Sometimes at night when we're afraid, singing to the Lord drives the fear from our lives.

Wherever you are—in bed, at school, or in the car—you can celebrate God's greatness in song. Even if you can't sing out loud, you can make music in your heart to the Lord. Feel free to enjoy Him. He is your song.

Thought to remember:
I can sing love songs to the Lord.

Additional verses:
Psalm 13:6; 28:7; 66:1–4; 98:1; 104:33; 149:5; 1 Chronicles 16:9

Have you ever driven by a field of giant sunflowers early in the morning and noticed that their faces are turned to the east? Everywhere you look, the arms of trees, the hands of plants, the faces of flowers are lifted to the sun.

Sunlight is life to plants. It's soaked up by leaves and turned into food for growth. Without sunshine most plants become pale and skinny instead of full and green. But we all know that plants are bound to the earth by their roots. They can't walk and they don't run. So how do they reach the sun?

They do the dance of the plants, a s-l-o-w ballet to bend and grow and twirl around, till life-giving light of the sun is found.

There's a word for the bending, twisting, and growing that plants do to move toward light. It's **phototropism,** and it means turning toward or away from light.

phototropism: (foe-TAHT-ruh-piz-um)

How does phototropism work?

Simple experiments done in the late 1800s give clues. First, foil collars that blocked out light were wrapped around the stems of seedlings where they bent toward light. The seedlings still pointed toward light, even though the part that bent was covered up.

In the second experiment, light-tight caps were fitted to the *tips* of these seedlings. The seedlings now behaved as if there were no light at all—they didn't bend. What did this experiment prove? Something in the tip of the seedlings sends a signal to the stem to tell it to bend.

What's in the tip?

hormone: (HORE-mone)

Plants have chemical messengers in them called **hormones**. One hormone, **auxin,** helps plants move toward light. Auxin moves from the tips of plants down to the rest of the plant. It concentrates in the shaded sides of the stems. This buildup of auxin affects the cells on the dark side of the stem, causing them to stretch and grow longer.

auxin: (AUK-sin)

> Blessed are those who have learned to acclaim you, who walk in the light of your presence, O Lord. They rejoice in your name all day long; they exult in your righteousness. For you are their glory and strength.
>
> PSALM 89:15–17a (NIV)

Light isn't the only thing plants move toward or away from. Their roots grow down into the ground in the direction of the pull of gravity. Grapevine branches and pea plants have **tendrils** (TEN-drulz) that respond to touch. These threadlike parts of plants wrap around something solid to hold up the vine. Some willow tree roots spread toward water.

EXPLORE IT!

Perhaps you've noticed. No matter which way you turn plants, they rotate to face the sun. Try this experiment with two or three house plants. Simply give them a twist until their leaves face slightly away from the sun. How long does it take for each plant to do an about-face? Do all plants do the twist?

DIG DEEPER!

* phototropism
* plants

The extra length makes plants bend toward light.

Everywhere you look, plants seek the light of the sun. We seek the light of the Son of God, Jesus. He is the Light of our lives.

Like plants, we are bound to this earth. When troubles shadow our lives, we can become skinny and unhealthy inside—like plants that struggle because they live in the shade.

That's why we need the light of the Son. Even though we can't see this light with our eyes, we can see it with our hearts. Moment by moment, we can turn our attention toward Jesus, the Light. When we do, we enjoy His love. We enjoy loving Him back. Being aware of His presence with us fills us with peace, hope, and comfort. Knowing that He's with us all day and all night brings us a wonderful joy that words can't describe. He scatters the shadows of our lives.

Sometimes we get distracted and focus on this world, others, or ourselves. This is like stepping back into the shadows. But God wants us to be in His light. He gently tells us when our eyes have turned away from Him. Turning back to Him brings us back into the joy of His light.

No matter where we are or what we're doing, we can turn the eyes of our hearts on the Son and bask in His light. Nothing makes life brighter.

Thought to remember:
I can live in the light of the Son, Jesus.

Additional verses:
Hebrews 12:2 (NIV); Psalm 105:4; 84:10–11a; 25:5 (NIV); Acts 2:25 (NIV)

32 IN a WORLD WitHout WORDS

Suppose we lived in a world without words. How would
we let our friends and families know what we needed or wanted?

Animals don't use words to talk. Yet they manage to pass information along to one
another about who they are, where they are, and what they want. What are some different ways that animals communicate? How about sound? Sounds are useful to animals that need to send messages quickly, over long distances, around obstacles, or in
the dark. The low groans and high squeals of humpback whales vibrate through ocean waters. Songs may
help whales stay in touch over long distances.

Animals also release chemicals called **pheromones**
to communicate. Like sounds, pheromones travel
around solid objects and are useful where there's little
light. But unlike sound waves, which travel quickly,
odors drift slowly through air and can last for days.

Female silk moths release pheromones to attract
males. Male moths catch the chemicals on feathery
antennae, then follow them to find the female. Worker bees warn hive members of
danger by giving off a chemical alarm signal. **Hyenas** mark out territories with long-lasting smells.

Some animals talk by touching. Touch lasts only for a moment and when animals
are near one another. Elephants twist their trunks together to say hello. Monkeys that
groom—or comb through—each other's hair fight less. Low-ranking monkeys may
groom higher-ranking monkeys to keep peace in the troop.

Another common way to communicate is through sight. A chimpanzee shows
anger, fear, and happiness by changing the look on its face. A dog communicates its
feelings through changes in the position of its ears, lips, mouth, body, and tail. An octopus speaks by changing colors. These signals are only useful if two animals are close
enough to see each other and if there's enough light.

Most animals talk to each other by sound, chemicals, touch, and sight, or a mix of
these. But electric fish communicate in a shocking way. These African fish send out
weak electric pulses to announce what species they belong to and whether they're male
or female. Electric signals are perfect for the dark, murky waters where these fish swim.

PHEROMONE:
(FEH-RuH-MOaN)
a chemical
released by an
animal that
PRoDuces a
ResPoNse iN
another animal
of the same kiND

HyeNa:
(Hi-EE-NuH) a
meat-eating
animal from
Africa with
SHoRt back
Legs

To DiScover
MORE about
wHat animals
Say wHeN tHey
communicate,
tuRN to "THe
MeSSage" ON
page 19.

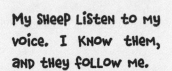
My sHeeP LiSteN to my
voice. I KNOW tHem,
and tHey foLLow me.

JOHN 10:27

Elephants bark, roar, trumpet, and growl. They also talk in deep rumbles too low for our ears to hear. These sounds travel long distances through forests and grasslands. Separated family groups rumble to communicate. Females also call to faraway males with this silent sound.

DISCOVER IT!

How would you communicate if you could not use words? Try this experiment with a group of friends or your family. Try to go without talking for at least an hour. What creative ways did you invent to talk to each other?

CHECK IT OUT!

Check out a library book on American Sign Language and learn signs to say the following phrases:

"Please."

"Thank you."

"I love you."

"How are you?"

"Fine."

DIG DEEPER!

★ how animals talk
★ animal language

All of these types of communication help animals live together in this world. Humans use all these, too—if you include email!

Have you ever thought about what it would be like to communicate with someone you've never seen, smelled, heard, or touched? At first this might seem impossible.

Unless that Someone is God. He communicates with our spirits.

How?

He "speaks" to us of His power and reveals who He is through the amazing world He created. No matter where we are, we listen when we take time to look at trees, flowers, and stars. Every time we see a rainbow, we hear God's promise.

Sometimes, we also "hear" God's still, small voice in our hearts. He might tell us how much He loves us, reveal something about himself, or even correct us. There's nothing more soothing than hearing God's gentle voice.

The Bible is a tool God uses to communicate with us, too. Through these written words, He teaches and guides us. Sometimes a verse stands out from all the others to encourage us.

Not only does God speak to us, but He "touches" us, as well. We're touched by His love when we first come to Him and He brings us into His family. His love touches us when we're cared for in special ways by others who belong to Him.

Communication is a two-way street, though, and God also wants us to talk to Him. It doesn't matter whether we speak out loud or whisper in our hearts. He hears it all. Talking to God is even better than talking to a best friend. That's how open and honest we can be.

Take time to communicate with God. Your love for Him will deepen as you do.

Thought to remember:

God wants me to communicate with Him.

Additional verses:

Genesis 9:12–15; Isaiah 50:4–5 (NIV); Psalm 19:1–4; 66:19; 1 Kings 19:11–13; Romans 1:20

When the sun sinks below the skyline, we know another day is coming to an end. Darkness spreads across the sky to swallow the day; stars sparkle, the moon shines. We seek the comfort of our homes to eat dinner, finish homework, and get ready for bed.

But for many animals, nighttime is the beginning of another day. While we slip into our beds, a parade of creatures rise and slip from their homes.

For many animals, the setting of the sun means cool night temperatures and moist air. For others, darkness provides a cover of safety as they search for food. But night also brings the need for animals to find other creatures in a realm without light.

Some snakes have heat-sensing pits below their eyes that detect prey. Male moths have feathery antennae they use to catch the chemicals of females. Some **nocturnal** animals have extra-sensitive eyes that pick up faint amounts of light.

Owls do. They have special eyes that, along with special ears, help them capture prey at night. These are oversized eyes. In fact, owl eyes are so large that there's little room for them to move in their sockets—which is why owls turn their heads instead. How would you like to be able to turn your head to look behind you?

Owls also have huge **pupils** that open wide to let in as much light as possible. Any light that enters the pupil falls on the **retina** at the back of the eye. In the retina are rods and cones. Rods are sensitive to small amounts of light; cones are designed to pick up detail and color. Which of these do you think night-flying owls have more of?

As you probably guessed, owls have many more rods than cones. Our eyes have more cones. This explains why an owl's eyes are about one hundred times more sensitive to light than ours.

Behind the retina is a layer called the **tapetum**. Like a mirror, the tapetum reflects back any light missed by the rods at the back of the eye. Have you seen the eyeshine of

nocturnal: (KNOCK-TUR-nul) animals that come out at night

To discover more about owl ears, turn to "Three Cheers for Ears" on page 86.

pupil: (PEW-pull) the round black part in the center of your eye. It controls the amount of light that enters your eye.

retina: (REH-tin-uh) the light-sensitive layer at the back of the eye

tapetum: (tuh-PEA-tum)

> Suppose I were to say, "I'm sure the darkness will hide me. The light around me will become as dark as night." Even that darkness would not be dark to you. The night would shine like the day, because darkness is like light to you.
>
> PSALM 139:11–12

Fish, shrimp, and grasshoppers that live in caves have eyes that are smaller than normal because there's little use for sight in a dark cave. Some cave dwellers have no eyes at all. Many sense their surroundings with long feelers.

EXPLORE IT!

The rods of our eyes are on the outer edges of the retina. The cones are concentrated in the middle. On a cloudless night, find a place *away from city lights*. First look directly at the stars. Next, turn your head so that the same stars are to the side of your face. Can you see the stars better when you look directly at them, or when the stars are to the side? Since light-sensitive rods are on the outside edges of our eyes, the stars will be brighter when you don't look directly at them.

CHECK IT OUT!

To see how the pupil of your eye expands and contracts with changes in light, you will need a mirror and flashlight. Shut off the lights in a room that has no windows. Wait in the dark for about a minute. Then, while looking into the mirror, turn on the flashlight and shine it near your eye (do not shine it directly in your eye!). As you bring the flashlight closer to your eye, what happens to your pupil? Does it become larger or smaller? Now aim the flashlight away from your face so that less light shines into your eye. Does your pupil expand to let in more light?

DIG DEEPER!

* night animals
* night creatures
* animal vision

animals at night? If so, you've seen light reflected by the tapetum.

For many animals, nighttime is lifetime. The special design of their senses makes it possible for them to feed and find mates when there's little light. Since we don't have owl eyes, it's hard for us to feel safe when surrounded by darkness. Not being able to see makes us feel unprotected. We imagine dangerous beasts lurking about, and this can make us afraid to be alone in the dark.

If this describes you, it's nothing to be embarrassed about—you're not the only one. You might be surprised to learn that there are many adults who are afraid of the dark, even when there's no reason to be fearful.

If you're ever afraid at night, it helps to know that even though you can't see through the darkness, there's someone with you who can. That someone is God. For God, the night shines like the day; it's the same as light to Him.

Whether you're in the light of day or dark of night, the Lord sees everything. He's the One who keeps you from harm. When you know that the Creator of day and night is with you, you can relax—you don't have to be afraid.

Thought to remember:

God sees through the darkness. He is with me.

Additional verses:

2 Samuel 22:29; Hebrews 4:13a; Psalm 91:5a; 23:4; Deuteronomy 31:6

34) A Special Place

Pack your gear—it's time for a trip to a tropical rain forest.
These jungles grow in a belt around the earth's middle. And even though they take up only a small amount of the earth's surface, more than half of the world's plant and animal species are thought to flourish there.

Rain forest trees are tall and wide. It would make sense that they'd have large roots that grow deep into the earth to support them. But that's not the case. Rain forest soils are poor. These giant trees have small roots that spread out just under the surface of the soil. They collect food from dead plants and animals that rot quickly in this hot, moist climate.

Take a look around. At first everything looks like a thick green tangle. But as we explore, we sort out individual plants and animals from this rich rain forest world. . . .

The forest floor is warmed least by the sun because light is blocked out by these tall trees. This is perfect for plants such as ferns, which need little light. The floor is also perfect for mammals that don't climb—**coatis**, **tapirs** . . . there's an armadillo over there. Keep an eye out for jaguars, too.

With the help of ropes, let's climb into the twilight world of the understory. Trees here are skinny. They have large leaves, designed to capture light. Plenty of birds, bats, spiders, frogs, and insects make their homes in this dim level. Iguanas, anteaters, **ocelots**, and three-toed **sloths** also hang out here.

Keep climbing, up into the canopy level, toward the light. The canopy, made of branches and leaves of tall trees, forms the roof of the rain forest. Most of the plants and animals of the forest live here.

Have a seat on one of these wide branches. But watch where you sit—they're crawling with ants . . . rats and bats . . . birds, beetles, and bright blue butterflies . . . mice and monkeys . . . frogs, lizards, snakes . . . and an occasional *two*-toed sloth. These are just a few of the animals that feast on flowers, fruits, berries—and each other!—at this level.

As you can see, each branch is also packed with a rich collection of plants, some

coati: (co-AH-tee) a raccoonlike creature, but with a longer nose and tail

tapir: (TAY-purr) a hoofed animal with a heavy body, short legs, and a long, fleshy nose

ocelot: (AWE-suh-lot) a medium-sized wildcat that has black stripes and spots

sloth: (slawth) a slow moving, bearlike animal that lives in trees

More tropical rain forest tidbits:

* These thick forests are always green.

* Up to two hundred inches of rain fall here each year.

* Many animals that live in these trees never touch the ground.

* The Amazon rain forest in South America is the largest in the world.

DIG DEEPER!

* tropical rain forest

that even grow on the leaves of others. Tiny worlds exist inside pineapple-shaped plants at this level of the rain forest. These plants, called **bromeliads**, collect water and dirt in the pockets between their leaves. They're miniponds and gardens that become home to many creatures—mosquitoes, spiders, tree frogs, worms, salamanders, and even small crabs. Plant and animal life can become so heavy that branches sometimes break from the weight.

bromeliad: (bro-ME-lee-add)

Before we get too comfortable, let's climb higher, into trees that stick up above the canopy. There are animals that live, eat, and breed way up here, too—nearly two hundred feet aboveground. Don't look down—you might get dizzy!

Trees up here have small, leathery leaves to protect against water loss from harsh winds and sunlight. That huge gray bird over there is a harpy eagle, the largest of eagles. It's on the lookout for squirrel monkeys. Do you hear that loud call? A howler monkey must have spotted the eagle, too.

The colorful flash that zipped by is a ruby-throated hummingbird. The mosquitoes are a bother up here, too, aren't they?

From the ground to the tops of the trees, plants and animals take advantage of different conditions at different levels. Everything from the itty-bittiest bacteria on the ground to the biggest bird at the top of the trees has a special place to live, a **habitat**.

habitat: the place where a plant or animal lives

Do you have a special place? This might be a rock where you can sit and look out over the city, a tree you can climb, or even a chair in a quiet corner of the living room. It's *your* place, a place where you can get away from the noise and busyness of life, where you retreat to find rest and peace, where you are strengthened, where you can be yourself. Perhaps this is where you think and dream; perhaps it's where you draw or read.

Even if we don't have a special rock, tree, or chair in the corner of the living room, when we belong to Jesus, we're in Him. He's our special place.

Whether we're alone or in the midst of a crowd of people, as we live in Jesus we have rest and peace, we're strengthened, and we can be ourselves. Whether we're sitting quietly or rushing around, in Jesus we find a sense of calm. He's our retreat.

Some species of rain forest plants and animals live only on one spot on one tree. But our special place in Jesus is different. Because we're always in Him, no matter where we go or what we do, we're in our special place.

Even when the world is like a tangled rain forest, Jesus is our special place.

Thought to remember:

Jesus is my special place.

Additional verses:

John 14:20; Colossians 2:9–10a; Philippians 4:19; Psalm 32:7a; 27:4–5; 61:4

FIND IT!

The names of many rain forest animals are as strange as the animals themselves. Find them in the word puzzle below. Names can be found forward, backward, up, down, and diagonally.

ANTEATER	GECKO	SLOTH
BEE	LEMUR	TAPIR
BOA	PANGOLIN	TERMITE
BUSH BABY	PARROT	TIGER
CHAMELEON	POISON-ARROW	TOUCAN
FROG	PYTHON	
FRUIT BAT	RED-EYED TREE FROG	

```
G O D A B O V E A L L G O D S
R H T M P A H T O L S B C Z T
G I E E P R T V T O R R A P L
E U P L N E B A A R P E H F R
C N K A S T M C B Y A L G I M
K A M T T A W E T T E V P I O
O C C E O E E H I M I D S L T
T U A B S T O M U Z I U C R E
P O I S O N A R R O W F R O G
F T W U P A N G O L I N V F A
G O R F E E R T D E Y E D E R
I P C S P N O E L E M A H C T
B U S H B A B Y E T I M R E T
```

 The answers are on page 152.

Animal ears come in several shapes and sizes.

They're round or pointy,
Short or tall,
Flat or floppy,
Big or small.

In spite of how different they look, ears have one main purpose. They're designed to catch sound. Picking up sounds helps animals escape predators, track down prey, locate mates, and find the way.

Sounds are created by vibrations. The vibrations travel in waves to the outer ear, where they're channeled to the eardrum and inner parts of the ear. From here the vibrations are transferred to the brain, where they're understood as sound.

Coyotes have large, pointy ears that channel sound to sensitive inner ears. Their hearing is so keen, coyotes can zero in on mice scurrying in grass or burrowing under snow.

Owls also have powerful hearing to pick up on prey. They have no outer ears—the tufts on their heads are only feathers. Instead, they have ear openings—or slits—on the sides of their heads, hidden by feathers. The left opening is higher than the opening on the right to help owls pinpoint the location of mice on the darkest of nights. To direct sound to these superduper ears, a ridge of feathers outlines the owl's face.

Insect-eating bats have an unusual sound system. Called **echolocation**, this system allows bats to find prey and avoid obstacles while flying in the dark. Here's how it works. Bats send out **ultrasound**, sounds *so* high-pitched that we can't hear them. These squeaks hit objects and bounce back to the bat. The direction from which these sounds return, and the speed with which they return, reveal the location of moths, trees, rocks, and more. The bat's large ears receive these echoes and send them on to the brain, allowing the bat to make high-speed changes to its flight path.

We can't hear bat ultrasound, but some moths can. The moth ear is a simple eardrumlike membrane found on both sides of the body, underneath the wings. Being alert to bat squeaks gives moths a chance to fly for their lives.

Like moths, crickets also have simple ears. Found on their front legs, cricket ears

> DOES HE WHO MADE THE EAR NOT HEAR?
>
> PSALM 94:9a

echolocation:
(ecK-OH-LOW-
KAY-SHUN)

ultrasound:
(UL-truH-SOUND)

consist of an eardrum and nerves. They're designed to allow female crickets to pick up the *ear*-resistible chirps of males.

Animals have different styles of ears, but the job description is always same—to sense the world of sound. Perhaps God gave ears to creatures just so we could understand what God means when He says that He hears us. We have no idea what His ears look like, but that's not what matters. What's important is the fact that He hears. God assures us over and over in the Bible that His ear is turned toward those who call to Him.

Perhaps you find it hard to believe that someone who can't be seen can hear you. But God can do anything. He created us to have a close relationship with Him, so He wants us to feel free to come to Him, to talk to Him.

God's ears are so powerful that He's tuned in to everything from the ultrasound whispers of our hearts to the loudest cries of our voices. God is all ears when it comes to listening to His children.

The only time God doesn't hear us is when we delight in sin. Then our prayers bounce back to our own ears, just as bat squeaks bounce back to theirs. But as quick as we turn from our sins, God's ears are open to us again.

There's no creature on earth with ears as good as God's. We can be sure that anytime, anyplace, He hears us.

Thought to remember:
God hears me.

Additional verses:
Isaiah 59:1; Micah 7:7; Psalm 18:6; 116:1–2 (NIV); 139:4; 66:18–19; 1 John 5:14; Philippians 4:6; 1 Thessalonians 5:17

African elephant ears are larger than those of any other animal. Does the size of their outer ears affect their ability to hear? In this case, outer ear size has to do with keeping cool. Heat is released through these gigantic floppy ears.

TRY IT!

Discover how the outer ear funnels sounds into the inner ear. Draw a large cone, or flat-topped triangle, on a piece of construction paper. The bottom side of the paper needs to be wider than the top. Cut out the shape.

Now roll the paper into the shape of a megaphone. Click on the radio. Standing about six feet away, turn one ear toward the radio and listen. Next, place the small end of the cone next to your ear and listen. Remove the tube and listen to the sounds again. What differences do you notice? Experiment with the size of the megaphone. How do changes in size affect your hearing? What happens if you put the large end of the cone up to your ear?

DIG DEEPER!
* animal ears
* hearing
* animal senses
* sounds

Have you ever needed help combing angry snarls out of your hair? Or tying your shoes? Do you fix all your meals and do all your own laundry?

Think about a normal day in your life. From the time you slide into your breakfast chair in the morning until you slip under your covers at night, how many times does somebody help you out?

Animals help each other, too. Let's go on a science safari to discover how.

Many animals help each other catch food. Male chimpanzees do. And they're willing to share food with those who beg from them. The same is true for African wild dogs. Without teamwork, these long-legged hunters wouldn't be able to bring down large prey. After the hunt, they carry food back for pups, mothers, and other adults who stayed behind. Even the sick and injured are cared for this way.

> **The Lord is with me; He is my helper.**
>
> PSALM 118:7 (NIV)

When in danger, animals also give each other a helping hoof—or wing or fin. Zebras and musk-oxen form fences between their young and predators. So do elephants. Florida scrub-jay guards warn family members about snakes. Chimpanzees come to each other's rescue when attacked by baboons or rival chimps. Dolphins lift injured dolphins to the surface so they don't drown.

Maybe you've baby-sat a younger brother, sister, or cousin. Elephants have baby-sitters, too. These baby-sitters are called "aunts"—they may really be aunts, but they might also be grandmothers, sisters, and cousins. Aunts help out in many ways. They use their trunks to lower tree branches for babies to eat and to push struggling babies up steep slopes. When a calf misbehaves, a whack from an aunt's trunk brings it back in line. Aunts watch over calves while they sleep and bring them back when they wander away.

Other species use baby-sitters, too. Wolves do. Young adult pack members play with and help feed wolf pups. Emperor penguin parents leave their children in nurseries while searching for food. Even Florida scrub jays have aunts and uncles—older brothers and sisters—who feed newly hatched young.

A special role for helpers develops when babies are orphaned. Female elephants and chimps may adopt motherless babies. African wild dog aunts *and* uncles have been known to look after orphaned pups. In one instance, a pack's only female died. Male dogs in the group brought food to the pups until they were old enough to join the hunt.

The most amazing example of animals helping others comes from **captive** chimpanzees. These apes can't swim and are afraid of water. When one young female fell into a water-filled **moat**, another chimp jumped a fence. Holding on to a clump of grass, she reached into the water and grabbed the drowning chimp's arm to save her life.

Helpers in the animal world add to the health and survival of individuals in the group. Helpers in our lives do, too. We depend on each other for everything from food to love.

God gives people to help us, but He is our greatest helper. As our Father, He takes care of us in ways far greater than any person can. That's the whole reason He came to earth in human form. Jesus understands how we feel when we go through hard times because He lived here in a human body.

While Jesus traveled the dusty roads of Israel, He helped many people. He helped so many people that the earth isn't big enough to hold the books that could be written about all the things He did. Then, when He went back to heaven, the Father sent the Holy Spirit to live inside us, to be our helper.

Like the aunts and uncles of the animal world, the Spirit feeds and teaches us and helps us up the steep slopes of life. He corrects and protects us. He looks after us when no one else is around. What a comfort it is to know that the Spirit of God is with us as we travel the trails of this earth.

Is there something that troubles your heart? No problem is too big—or too small—for God. Just ask for His help. He holds your hand and says, "Don't be afraid. I will help you."

Can you think of animal helpers that live in our homes? Blind people depend on guide dogs to lead them through this world. Dogs are also trained to be ears for the deaf, and legs and hands for those who use wheel chairs. Cats, dogs, and birds in our homes help us every day through their companionship, too.

LIST IT!

Sometimes we don't even notice the help God gives us. Find a quiet spot and ask the Lord to open your eyes to the ways He has helped you. Then wait for Him to reveal His works in your life. Make a list of the things He brings to mind. Give God thanks for all He has done.

Thought to remember:
God is my Helper.

Additional verses:
Isaiah 41:13; Psalm 72:12; 121:1–2; Hebrews 4:15–16; 2 Samuel 22:30

DIG DEEPER!
★ animal helpers
★ animal behavior

37. Rest Easy and Sleep Like a Log

Sometimes you love it, sometimes you hate it. When you're having a sleepover, going to bed seems like such a waste.

But when you reach the end of a long, tiring day, it's a relief to drop into bed.

Whether you love it or hate it, sleep is something everyone needs. And humans aren't alone.

Sloths are the original couch potatoes. They sleep away twenty hours of every day. Armadillos need slightly less—about nineteen hours.

At the other end of the scale are elephants and dolphins. They get by on four to five hours of ZZZs per day.

What's so important about sleep?

No one knows for sure. For many animals, sleep may be a way to save energy. It may be a time for body repairs and growth, a time to restore strength. Some scientists also think that sleep helps renew the brain, allowing it to process information and get it ready for another day.

Where animals make themselves comfortable for the night—or day—varies. Some, like you, sleep in beds. That's true for gorillas. They bend handfuls of branches and plants over to form simple platforms. Raccoons hole up inside trees during the day. Hedgehogs build nests of dead leaves, hidden in the arms of tree roots.

Manatees snooze upside down, near the floor of the ocean. Sea otters rest on their backs on the surface of the water, wrapped in beds of seaweed to keep from drifting away. Giant pandas nap anytime of the day or night, but usually after eating, near dawn and dusk. They simply curl up or spread out on the ground. Sometimes they doze against trees, hunched over, chins rested on chests.

Birds sleep perched on branches. Or they snooze on the ground. You may have seen a bird balanced on one leg, head tucked under its wing.

Fish look like they're sleeping when they float head down or on their sides. But their lack of action isn't considered real sleep. Insects don't seem to sleep at all. They only rest between periods of activity.

Wherever they sleep or rest, most animals must keep an eye out for enemies. For

Manatee: (MAN-uh-tee) a large plant-eating mammal that lives in the water. It has flippers and a face similar to a walrus.

When fish rest, they don't close their eyes. They can't—they don't have eyelids!

> I will lie down and sleep in peace. Lord, you alone keep me safe.
>
> PSALM 4:8

that reason, sleep is often light and caught in snatches. Some hoofed animals only doze while others around them stand guard. Ducks that try to get shut-eye at the edge of a flock sleep with one eye open. Lions, on the other hand, don't worry about predators. They don't have to. After a large meal, they may hit the sack for two or three days straight.

Although scientists don't fully understand what role sleep plays in the daily lives of animals and humans, they do understand that it's necessary. Rats starved of sleep lose weight and die. Humans kept awake for two days have trouble thinking clearly. After three days, sleep-hungry humans develop problems with seeing, speaking, and hearing. They **hallucinate.**

hallucinate: (HuH-LOO-siH-Nate) to See things that aren't Real

As much as our bodies and minds need sleep, there are some nights when we're wide awake. We lie motionless in bed, hoping to sink into the world of dreams, but our minds won't quit. Without the activities of the day to distract us, troubles and fears turn to monsters. *Did I do okay on the math test? Oh no—I forgot to read the science pages! Will Coach let me play in tomorrow's game? Why is Dad mad at me? What was that sound? Is someone breaking into the house? I miss my dog.* These are the types of thoughts that make our hearts race and cause us to toss and turn.

How do we let go of our fears? How do we turn our attention away from troubles that can't be solved in the middle of the night?

One way is to pray about them. God never sleeps. We can be sure that day or night, He watches over us and cares for us as a parent cares for a child. Turning our worries and fears over to Him causes us to rest, brings us peace—and sleep!

Another solution is to pray for others. With our minds turned away from ourselves, we drift off to dreamland. And the next thing we know, it's time to get up.

Trusting the One who never sleeps brings us the sweetness of sleep.

Thought to remember:
God watches over me day and night. He never sleeps.

Additional verses:
Psalm 3:5; 121:2–4 (NIV); Philippians 4:6–7; Isaiah 26:3 (NIV); Proverbs 3:5–6

How do scientists define sleep? When an animal sleeps, it
* takes a resting or relaxed position
* shows a lack of activity
* becomes less aware of its surroundings but is easily awakened
* shows brain-wave patterns that are much different than when it's awake

Parrot fish don't rest in nests, but they do surround themselves in blankets. At night many types of parrot fish swim to a safe spot and produce a slimy bubble that envelopes them. This bubble is like the bubble of protection Jesus wraps us in while we sleep.

CHECK IT OUT!

How do animals sleep? Visit a pet store and see for yourself. Do they sleep sitting up or lying down? Do they sleep out in the open or in hidden places? Do they snooze alone or close to others? Are their eyes open or closed?

DIG DEEPER!
* how animals sleep
* sleep
* ways animals rest

Heart of Pearls

You know how it feels to have a rock trapped between your foot and shoe. Even a tiny rock creates a lot of pain. First you try to jiggle it to one side. Or tap it to the toe. With each step, your foot screams for you to get rid of that rock. Until . . . you finally take off your shoe and empty it of **irritation**! An irritation is just how a pearl gets started.

Within the crusty shell of a pearl oyster lies its soft, fleshy body. Surrounding this body is a skin called a **mantle**. The mantle produces mother-of-pearl, a silvery material that lines the shell. A grain of sand, a small piece of shell, or a tiny parasite trapped between the shell and mantle irritates the oyster in the same way a rock bothers your foot.

But an oyster has no hands to get rid of irritations. So what does it do? The mantle coats the grit with layers of mother-of-pearl. Over several years, the painful speck is transformed into a smooth pearl.

Pearls produced naturally by oysters aren't usually round and perfectly smooth as are most of the pearls you've seen. In the early 1900s man discovered a way to increase the number of round pearls. To make a **cultured** pearl, a pearl farmer operates on an oyster. First, the halves of an oyster's shell are slightly spread apart. Next, a cut is made in the body of the oyster. A sliver of mantle from another oyster is slid into this cut. The pearl farmer then plants a small round bead next to it. The bead is the irritation that the extra piece of mantle coats with mother-of-pearl.

These seeded oysters are kept in large baskets in the sea. From time to time they're plucked from the water, cleaned, and X-rayed. Three years later when the shell is finally pried open, what does the pearl farmer find?

> *Gift of an oyster,*
> *Full moon of quiet color—*
> *Beauty born of pain.*

irritation: (ear-ih-TAY-shun) something that bothers you

mantle: (MAN-tul)

Another word for mother-of-pearl is nacre (NAY-kur).

cultured: (CUL-churd) made by man

> [Now] for a little while you may have had to suffer grief in all kinds of trials. These have come so that your faith—of greater worth than gold, which perishes even though refined by fire—may be proved genuine and may result in praise, glory and honor when Jesus Christ is revealed.
>
> 1 PETER 1:6a–7(NIV)

The seed of a pearl is an irritation that causes the oyster pain. We also have irritations in our lives, such as problems with families or friends, or challenges in school. Perhaps we have physical problems. Maybe we don't like the way we look. How do we greet the troubles that come into our lives?

At first we probably try to get rid of the grit or run from it. Maybe we even try to ignore it. These are natural things to do. Nobody likes pain.

But God uses pain in our hearts.

People with problems flocked to Jesus when He walked on earth. Today our problems still cause us to turn to Him. When we go to God with our hurts, He comforts us. As the oyster coats an irritation with mother-of-pearl, God coats our pain with His love. In Him we find strength and patience that enable us to keep going. Our faith is strengthened. We get to know God in a much deeper way.

The mother-of-pearl that coats a shell is present before an irritation gets trapped inside. But when it turns an irritation into a polished gem, the mother-of-pearl is revealed in a more beautiful way. Pain also reveals the beauty of Jesus in our lives. He changes the pain in our hearts to pearls.

Thought to remember:

Jesus can turn pain into something beautiful.

Additional verses:

Habakkuk 3:17–19; Isaiah 61:3; Romans 5:3–5; 8:38–39

At first glance most pearls look white. But if you look carefully, you'll see that many pearls have a pink, gold, or creamy tint.

There are also black, silver-gray, and dark green pearls. These are found in oysters that live off the west coast of Australia. Not only are they unusual in color, but also in size. Some black pearls are much larger than white ones.

EXPLORE IT!

Use an onion to see how layers of mother-of-pearl form a pearl. To begin, peel off the outer, papery skin. Continue to peel the onion, layer by layer, until you get to the middle. Like the onion, a pearl is formed of many layers.

WRITE IT!

Try your hand at a **haiku** (HY-koo) about nature, like the one on the bottom of page 92. A haiku is a type of Japanese poem, often written about nature or seasons. There are three unrhymed lines. The first line usually has five syllables, the second has seven, and the third has five.

DIG DEEPER!

* pearls
* shells
* oysters

39 Living Water

If you were stranded by yourself in a desert of hot sand, what would you want with you? Your parents? An air conditioner? Water—*lots* and *lots* of water to quench your thirst?

Desert animals need water just as every living thing does. But what makes a desert a land of sand is lack of water. How do dwellers of dry places get enough H_2O? They have some strange ways. . . .

First they have to find it. Many, like kangaroo rats, may never even sip a bit of liquid. Their bodies make it as they process the foods they eat. Body fluids from prey are a source of water for some predators. Some roaches and desert ticks absorb water from the air.

Other creatures of the **Namib** Desert in Africa harvest water from fogs that veil the sand dunes. Button beetles build tiny ridges of sand. Once the ridges are soaked, these round beetles suck water from them. A Namib gecko simply waits in the fog while water gathers on its body. Then the gecko licks its head and eyes to quench its thirst. The head-stander beetle crawls to the top of the dunes and sticks its hind end into the fog. Water droplets form on the back of this black beetle and roll down to its mouth.

Finding water is one problem, but keeping it is another. How do desert animals preserve precious water?

For some this means staying out of the sun during the hottest part of the day. Insects, spiders, snakes, and small mammals hide from the heat under the sand or in cool, moist burrows. Many are nocturnal—they surface only in the chill of night. Larger animals such as jackrabbits wait in the shade of bushes or rock ledges. But camels are too big for burrows, and there may not be any trees for shade. What do they do?

Camels have custom bodies built to beat the heat. Their coats are tan, the color of sand. Pale colors reflect the hot rays of the sun. Their coats are thick to keep heat out.

H_2O: (AITCH-two-OH) a scientific way to say water

Namib: (NUH-MIB)

To discover more about how animals control their body temperatures, turn to "Cool It" on page 28.

Jesus stood up and spoke in a loud voice. He said, "Let anyone who is thirsty come to me and drink. Does anyone believe in me? Then, just as Scripture says, streams of living water will flow from inside him."

JOHN 7:37b–38

Fur on their bellies is thinner to *let* heat out. Camels store fat in their humps instead of all over, because fat traps heat.

When we get hot, we sweat. Dogs pant. But sweating and panting use up water. Camels and other desert dwellers can't afford to lose water, so they sweat only after their temperatures rise several degrees. Their bodies are able to store heat until nighttime temperatures drop again.

Another way for camels and kangaroo rats to save water is to recycle moisture in their breath before it leaves their noses. They flush out body wastes in small amounts of urine. The droppings of kangaroo rats are nearly dry.

Animals that live in dry places satisfy their thirst in extraordinary ways, don't they?

Humans have the need to satisfy two types of thirst. One is the physical thirst that we satisfy with water. But the other is spiritual. For that we need an extraordinary way to satisfy our thirst—and it doesn't involve a faucet. It's an extraordinary person named Jesus. He's the living water. He satisfies the thirst we have in our hearts for God. It's a thirst that nothing and no one else can satisfy.

Like the animals of the desert, we must find this living water. Many of us spend our days searching for it in places it doesn't exist. Have you ever thought that if only you could be more popular, or the star of the ball team, or if only you had better clothes or the latest video game, you would be happy? We all think this way at some time or another, hoping these things will satisfy our inner thirst.

But when Jesus lived on earth, He told a woman at a well that if she drank the water He gave her, she would never thirst again. Anything other than Jesus satisfies only for the moment. That's why we lose interest in a pair of shoes after we buy them, why winning one tournament isn't enough, and why we can feel empty after opening all our presents at Christmas. Trying to satisfy our thirst for God with things from this world would be like a head-stander beetle trying to quench its thirst with oil. It doesn't work!

Once we drink the living water, our search is over. We never thirst again. Then we can live and be refreshed, even in a desert land.

Thought to remember:

Only Jesus can satisfy the thirst of my heart.

Additional verses:

Psalm 42:1–2; John 4:10–14; 6:35; Isaiah 49:10; 41:17–18; Colossians 2:9–10

Some desert frogs and toads go underground to stay cool. Frogs easily lose moisture through their skin, so they must burrow into mud to keep from drying out. Here they rest until the next rain—which may take several days or *years*—before they resurface to feed and mate.

DISCOVER IT!

See for yourself how you lose moisture when you breathe out. Hold a mirror in front of your mouth. Now breathe onto the mirror with a "huff." Do you see your breath on the mirror? This is moisture that you lose every time you exhale.

TRY IT!

Do pale colors really absorb less heat from the sun than dark ones? Put on a light-colored shirt and stand in the sun for a few minutes. Touch the material. How does it feel? Now change into a dark-colored shirt and stand in the sun. Again, touch the material. Does dark material absorb more heat than pale material?

DIG DEEPER!

* desert
* desert animals
* ecology

Picture a world where everyone looks the same, thinks the same, likes the same food, and lives in the same type of house. What kind of world would that be? Differences make our world fun and interesting, don't they?

In the world of plants and animals, differences can mean life or death. That's because similar creatures compete with each other for food and space. To reduce competition, every species holds a different position in the community of plants and animals where it lives. This position is called a **niche**. The niche is an animal or plant's "job" in life, including how it gets food and raises its young, and how its life affects the lives of others around it.

To get an idea about how animals compete with each other, think about your own home. Suppose you have one brother. Every morning you rise at six and head for the shower. Your brother gets up at six-thirty. By then the bathroom is free, and you're eating breakfast.

Now suppose your uncle comes to stay for a while. He gets up a few minutes before six and heads for the bathroom to shower and shave. He's still there at six when you need to take a shower. You'll be late for school. What do you do? Reverse your schedule and aim for the kitchen. But your uncle finished off your favorite cereal during a midnight snack. What do you do? Reach for the skillet and fry two eggs. By the time breakfast is over, it's almost six-thirty. Uncle is out of the bathroom and it's your turn. When your brother gets up, he'll have to change his schedule, too, because you've taken his niche in the bathroom.

In a similar way, animals compete for **resources** where they live. One species of warblers, which are small birds, eats insects in evergreen trees. But this warbler has competition—other types of insect-eating warblers. In order to live together in the same habitat, warbler number one eats insects in the lower branches and nests in the first weeks of June. Warbler number two eats insects in the middle branches and nests

NICHE: (NITCH)

RESOURCE: (RE-SORSE) a supply that can be used when needed

To discover more about animals and their habitats, turn to "A Special Place" on page 83.

> GOD MADE US. He created us to belong to Christ Jesus. Now we can do good things. Long ago God prepared them for us to do.
>
> EPHESIANS 2:10

at the end of July. A third warbler species might capture insects at the tips of the upper branches and nest in the last part of June and early part of July.

These birds survive because they live and eat in different places and have their young at different times. Like all plants and animals of the world, each has a niche.

So do you. God delights in how He made you, and He has special plans for you. These plans might be much different than what He designed for others around you, such as your best friend. Your niche might be in the upper branches of life; your friend's might be on the ground. Everything from the outside to the inside—your looks, personality, talents, strengths, and weaknesses—make you able to fulfill God's purposes for your life.

But even though different is good, do you ever worry about not fitting in at school or with your friends? Are you afraid others might not accept or like you because you're different?

Most people worry about this at some time or another. But if you look carefully, you'll notice that *everyone* is different in some way. When we understand that we're made one of a kind because God has a good purpose for us, we can relax and accept ourselves. We don't have to worry. We can enjoy being the way we are and get excited about our niche in this tree of life. Then we can accept others and their differences, too.

After all, if we all looked the same, thought the same, liked the same food, and lived in the same houses, what kind of world would this be?

Thought to remember:
God made me one of a kind for a good reason!

Additional verses:
Jeremiah 29:11 (NIV); Psalm 139:13–14; 16:5–6 (NIV); Isaiah 43:7b; 1 Timothy 4:4a

Have you ever heard it said that someone is "in his niche"? What does that mean? Someone is in his niche when it seems as if he's made for a job. Another way to say this is that an activity "fits" someone, like a shoe fits a foot. For example, one student might enjoy spending hours exploring computers. Another student might come alive while performing in front of a large group. Still another might be a natural talking to anyone. In each case, that person is in his or her niche.

LIST IT!

Grab paper and a pencil and find a quiet spot. Ask the Lord to open your eyes to the special things about yourself. List the things that come to mind. Here are some ideas. . . .

Do you have a big smile that welcomes others? What activities do you especially enjoy? Is it easy for you to talk to people, or do you prefer to be by yourself? Perhaps you're comfortable either way. Do you have a soft heart for others? Do you like to organize things? Are you an out-of-doors person? Perhaps you'd rather be inside, talking on the phone. When your list is complete, thank God for how He made you.

DIG DEEPER!

* ecology
* animal survival

41 WHaT'S FoR DinneR?

When your stomach grumbles—really grumbles—
what favorite food do you reach for? Pizza? Spaghetti? Broccoli?
Everyone knows that food is important to life. We need food for energy and food
for growth. So do animals. But unlike humans, animals don't fill their stomachs with
pizza, spaghetti, or broccoli. What foods *do* they eat when they're hungry as bears?

Many animals eat only plants. They're called **herbivores**. The cell walls of plants
are hard to **digest**, though. These tough walls must be
broken down before nutrients locked inside can be
used. To solve this problem, elk, cattle, and related
hoofed animals depend on bacteria to break down cell
walls.

When grasses and shrubs are eaten, they're first
stored in a large stomachlike sac. Here, bacteria start to
digest the food. Later, these partially digested plants
are brought up and chewed a second time. That's what
it means to "chew the cud." This process allows animals
to live on plants.

Koalas also carry **microscopic** critters in their stomachs. Scientists have found that
young koalas receive helpful bacteria by eating partially digested food from their
mothers.

You can probably think of many animals that eat plants. But what about animals
that eat only meat? These are called **carnivores**. Some predators ambush their dinner—they hide and wait patiently for prey to wander by. Camouflage and patience are
needed to surprise other animals. One type of crab spider blends in with flowers by
changing colors. It waits without moving until an insect comes close enough to be
grabbed.

Other hungry creatures not only wait for food, but use traps to snare supper. One
of the strangest trappers is the archerfish. This fish waits below the surface of the water
until a bug lands on a plant above it. Taking aim, the archer shoots a shower of water
bullets that knock the insect into the water.

Other predators hunt for food. Many use speed to chase down dinner. Cats sneak
up on prey. Owls have special feathers to make their flight silent. Once caught, their

---

herbivore:
(ER-buh-vore)

digest:
(die-JEST)
to break down
food so it can
be used by the
body

microscopic:
(my-cro-
SKAWP-ik)

carnivore:
(CAR-nih-vore)

To discover
more about
animals that
use camou-
flage, turn to
"Color
Changers" on
page 124.

> "My food," said Jesus,
> "is to do the will of
> Him who sent me and
> to finish His work."
>
> JOHN 4:34 (NIV)

prey is swallowed whole. Parts that can't be digested—bones, feathers, and fur—are coughed up later in pellets.

OMNIVORE:
(OM-NUH-VORE)

Omnivores eat plants and meat. Raccoons hunt for anything from frogs, fish, and crayfish to nuts, fruits, and seeds. They're not picky eaters.

Humans aren't picky, either. Most of us are also omnivores and, as we all know, will eat all kinds food to quiet the rumbles in our stomachs.

Humans have another type of hunger—one that animals don't have. Inside each of us is a spirit that hungers for closeness with God. For this we need spiritual food for spiritual energy and growth. Sometimes we try to feed this hunger with physical things from the world. Toys, clothes, and seeking popularity are a few ways we try to satisfy ourselves. But these things don't get rid of spiritual hunger pains.

So how do we feed our hungry hearts?

When Jesus walked on earth, He told the disciples that His food was to do the will of the Father who sent Him. Jesus' whole desire was to finish the work God had for Him to do. His work was to love us by caring for us unselfishly and putting our lives before His own.

When we're followers of Jesus, His life is inside of us. As Jesus obeyed the Father while He walked on earth, He now wants to obey the Father through each of us. God's will for us is the same as it was for Jesus—to look out for others in a helpful, unselfish way. Even when the path isn't easy, Jesus is our courage to follow through. When we offer God our willing hearts and hands for Him to love through us, we will know His love in a deeper way. God's love satisfies our souls as the best of foods satisfies our bodies.

Thought to remember:
Obedience to God satisfies my heart, like food satisfies my stomach.

Additional verses:
John 14:21, 23; 15:10 13; Luke 12:23; Psalm 63:3–5 (NIV)

When you want a snack, do you reach for fruit or chips or candy? If you lived in South Africa, you might enjoy the nutty taste of dried termites. In China you might dine on a bowl of water beetles soaked in ginger and soy sauce. Mmm. Tasty. Or if you're from Cambodia, deep-fried tarantulas might hit the spot.

LIST IT!

What do you reach for when you're hungry? For a whole day, write down *every* food you eat. Include a general idea of amounts (ex: two bowls of cereal). What types of foods make up the largest part of your diet? Are you surprised at your findings?

At the end of the day, also write down the spiritual food you ate. Here are some examples: offering to set the table, cleaning up your room, giving to someone in need. If your list is skinny, offer God your willing heart and hands. Expect Him to love through you.

DIG DEEPER!

* what animals eat
* animal hunters

Do you live where seasons change throughout the year?

If so, would you wear sandals, shorts, and sleeveless shirts in a blizzard? Would you wear a heavy jacket and snow pants in ninety-degree heat? Of course not! We all change clothes with the seasons.

So do trees with leaves. We know fall is here when gold, orange, and ruby-red leaves drip from trees like jewels. When cold winds snatch leaves from branches and trees stand clothed in white, we know we're gripped in the fist of winter. Then the earth warms and spring is here. Suddenly the whole world is dressed in a veil of green. Deep greens of summer will soon be on their way.

How do trees change with the seasons?

For a tree, spring is a time of waking from winter's sleep. Buds—produced on branches in the fall and **dormant** throughout the winter—now unfold as baby leaves and branches. Inside each leaf is a green substance called **chlorophyll** that helps make food for the tree. Chlorophyll works with sunlight, water, and air to produce a special sugar the tree uses to live and grow. While a tree makes food, it also begins the important job of making flowers.

Spring passes into summer. Above ground, the tree grows larger and taller. Below ground, roots lengthen. The green color of leaves deepens. Seeds develop inside fruit. By the end of summer, seeds are scattered.

As autumn approaches, some energy is stored in the trunk and roots for the winter; some is channeled into next year's growth. Tiny leaves and branches—and in some cases, flowers—are curled tightly inside bud cases that protect them during the winter. Days shorten and turn crispy cold. Since trees need sunlight and water to make food, production slows down, then stops altogether. As food production slows, the amount of chlorophyll in each leaf decreases. Gold, yellow, and orange—colors that were present in the leaves all along, but masked by chlorophyll—are now

> **Jesus Christ is the same yesterday and today and forever.**
>
> HEBREWS 13:8

DORMANT: (DOR-munt) not active, asleep

CHLOROPHYLL: (KLORE-uh-fill)

Trees and shrubs that flower in the spring form flower buds the fall before. Those that flower later—in the summer or fall—bloom off of new growth produced the same year.

Gold, yellow, and orange colors are present in leaves all summer. Deep reds and purples are formed in the fall, though. As weather cools, a layer of cells cuts the leaf off from the branch. Sugars inside leaves are trapped. Sunlight, plus cool nighttime temperatures, then form reds, rusts, and purples.

exposed. Soon after leaves change colors, they fall. Why? Trees lose water through their leaves. To prevent water loss during winter months when water is scarce, trees shed their leaves. Now trees rest, living off stored food. On the outside, it may look like nothing is going on. But there's life in the trunk, roots, and branches. New buds are on the branches waiting for spring, when the cycle begins again.

Trees change with the seasons. We change with the seasons of our lives.

There are springs, times of newness. Our lives are fresh and bursting with life, full of hopes, dreams, and expectations. God brings new growth into our lives. He prepares us to bear fruit.

There are summers, times of growth and increase. Our lives are full with laughter and activity. Our roots in Jesus grow, we're strengthened, and we bear fruit.

There are autumns. Just as trees lose their leaves in the fall, we also can go through times of loss. Perhaps we've been uprooted and had to move far away from everything we're familiar with. Perhaps a parent leaves, we lose a close friendship, or there's even a death. Cold winds of change whirl through our lives, bringing pain and, sometimes, confusion.

Then there are winters, times of difficulty. The skies of our lives may seem cold and dark. Perhaps we're stuck in sadness and tears, and it seems as if winter will go on forever. God may feel far away.

No matter what season we're in, it's good to remember that changes in our lives are normal. We can count on Jesus to be with us through them all. We live in a world of changes, but God never changes. He is always there for us. Through fun times, easy times, tough times, and sad times, Jesus' love is steady. No matter what season we're in, we can rejoice and have hope and peace because God always stays the same.

Thought to remember:

Changes in our lives are normal, but God never changes. His love is always with us.

Additional verses:

Ecclesiastes 3:1–8 (NIV); Hebrews 1:10–13; 13:8; Habakkuk 3:17–18; Deuteronomy 31:8

Are you suffering through a long, cold winter in your life? Perhaps a best friend has turned his or her back on you. Perhaps your family moved and you had to leave behind your friends. Perhaps your parents have problems or you've lost a family member. . . .

The buds of some trees don't open in spring unless they go through a period of cold winter temperatures.

The winter you're experiencing now will produce life in you later. And though the hope of spring may seem faraway, the Lord can be your sunny skies in the midst of a winter season.

CHECK IT OUT!

Check out the trees in your neighborhood.

If it's spring, have the buds opened? Which trees now have flowers?

If it's summer, are the leaves large and deep green? Can you tell where seeds are developing?

If it's fall, have the leaves begun to turn? Can you see where chlorophyll has faded? Are leaves falling? Can you find moon-shaped scars where leaves were once attached?

If it's winter, have all the leaves fallen? Can you find buds that are ready to burst open in the spring?

DIG DEEPER!

* how leaves change
* trees

43 More Than Sparrows

When you hear the word **desert**, what do you think of?

Hot? Dry? Cactus? Camels? Kangaroo rats? Sand?

You may have thought of different plants or animals, but you probably didn't think of rain or penguins, polar bears or pine trees. Certain plants and animals belong in certain areas of the world, don't they? Where they live depends on temperature, rainfall, and sunlight.

Wherever similar temperatures and amounts of rainfall and sunlight are found, similar plants and animals are also found—all over the world. These areas are divided into zones—called **biomes**.

biome: (BY-ome)

Let's play the biome game. What words come to your mind when you think of a tropical rain forest?

Do the words *hot, wet,* or *tall trees* come to mind? Do you think of boas? Big bats? Butterflies? How about parrots, monkeys, or jaguars? Rain forests stretch in a band around the earth's middle. Because there are no real seasonal changes here, many plants and animals thrive in the moist air and warm temperatures.

temperate (TEM-per-ut) having a mild climate, not extreme

Here's another biome: forests populated by trees that lose their leaves in the fall. They are called **temperate deciduous** forests. Did you think of any of these—deer, bears, rabbits, hedgehogs, squirrels, or red foxes? Woodpeckers or owls? These are just a few of many animals that find homes in deciduous woodlands. They're spread over the world in regions with hot summers, cold winters, and medium amounts of rain.

deciduous: (DIH-SID-you-us) trees that lose their leaves in the autumn. Perhaps you've raked oak, elm, maple, or birch leaves in the fall.

What comes to mind when you hear the word *grasslands*?

Tall grasses, antelope, prairie dogs? Add coyotes, snakes, and hawks to that list, too. Summers are hot and winters are cold where the deer and the antelope play. But there's not enough rain for trees to grow.

Other grasslands called **savannas** have a sprinkling of trees and shrubs. Warm year round with a long dry spell, the most famous savannas are in Africa and Australia. Short trees and long grasses grow here. What are some savanna animals? Zebras, chee-

savanna: SuH-VAN-uH

> He who did not spare his own Son, but gave him up for us all—how will he not also, along with him, graciously give us all things?
>
> ROMANS 8:32 (NIV)

HARE: SPRING HARES
LIVE IN AFRICA. THEY
LOOK LIKE GIANT
GERBILS.

tahs and giraffes. Lions and rhinos and **hares**—oh my! Elephants and kangaroos, too.

Let's move on to another forest—the evergreen forest. Perhaps pictures of pine trees, snow, bears, deer, moose, or elk fill your imagination. In these lands of long winters and short summers, evergreen trees are shaped to shed heavy snows from their branches. They don't lose their leaves in winter, either, so they can collect sunlight all year. The waxy covering on evergreen needles protects from water loss.

TUNDRA: (TON-DRUH)

The last biome is the **tundra**. Here are some clues: cold temperatures, lingering winters, hurried summers. Lichen, mosses, miniplants, grasses, and shrubs grow under these conditions. In the summer, only a top layer of soil thaws. Below this is permafrost—soil in permanent deep freeze. Wolves, caribou, snowy owls, arctic hares, and foxes live here, along with mosquitoes and flies that cloud the summer skies.

From dry deserts to wet rain forests, scientists have discovered a pattern. Similar plants and animals live and have their young in the same biomes all over the earth. Different temperature, rainfall, and sunlight combinations work together to support various types of life. But there's also something—someone—else at work creating conditions perfect for the animals that live there. Can you guess who that someone is?

Psalm 104 goes into detail about God's care for animals. He provides water for the beasts of the field and places for birds to build their nests. He brings forth grasses to feed cattle. High mountains shelter wild goats. The oceans are also full of creatures God watches over. All living creatures look to God for food, and He opens His hands to feed them with good things.

Why does God take care of living creatures?

Because He loves all that He has created. He makes it clear that all living things—even daisies and tiny sparrows—are important to Him.

But you are even more valuable to God than these . . . much more valuable. You are worth the life of His Son, Jesus. God refused to spare the life of Jesus, who was dear to His heart, so that you and He could be close.

The Arctic and Antarctic—areas around the North and South Poles—support animals such as penguins, polar bears, and seals. But they're not considered biomes because plants don't grow in these harsh lands of ice.

If you travel from the base to the top of a mountain, you will travel through several life zones. That's because weather conditions change with **altitude** (AL-tih-tude). The base might be a tropical rain forest. As you climb in altitude, the rain forest gives way to a deciduous forest. This changes to an evergreen forest, and tundra is near the top. The very top might be covered with ice, which is similar to the Arctic and Antarctica.

What biome do you live in? Ask yourself these questions and record your answers to discover which biome you live in.

What is the weather like in the summer and winter?

How much rain do you get every year?

Make a list of the types of trees, birds, animals, and insects that live where you do.

Even if you live in the center of the city surrounded by tall buildings, the weather and types of plants and animals in your area will give you some clues.

WRITE IT!

Read Psalm 104. Write down the ways that God cares for His creation. Now write down all the ways— big and little—that God takes care of you. Let Him know how you appreciate all He does.

DIG DEEPER!

* biomes
* ecology

That kind of care is more than any of us can grasp. But it does make it easy for us to understand that if He loves us that much, He will also look after all our needs.

The biomes of the world remind us that the Lord cares for all He has created. Even more, they help us understand how much He loves and cares for each of us.

Thought to remember:

Even more than the sparrow and the daisy, God takes care of me.

Additional verses:

Psalm 145:15–17; 147:8–9; 136:25; Matthew 10:29–31; Philippians 4:19

The Wise Gardener

Once upon a time there was a gardener who wanted to grow grapes. First he dug a wide hole in a sunny spot in his garden. Carefully he lowered the roots of a grapevine into their new home and covered them with soil. The vine itself wasn't much to look at—not much more than a thin brown stick with a few buds.

The first summer the plant grew taller. It sprouted tender branches. Then the chill of fall blew in; the vine slept through the long winter months.

In the spring of the second year, before the vine began to grow, the wise gardener visited his vine. One by one, he **pruned** off each branch until only a single sturdy trunk remained. That summer the trunk grew tall enough to reach a strand of wire the gardener had stretched out above the vine. Many new arms sprouted from the plant. Once again the gardener brought out his pruning shears. The gardener cut away all but two side branches—one arm extended to the right and another extended to the left. These he tied loosely to the wire. When the trunk reached a second horizontal wire, again he trained a branch out to each side and snipped off the top.

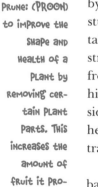

PRUNE: (PROON) to improve the shape and health of a plant by removing certain plant parts. This increases the amount of fruit it produces.

> [Jesus said,] "I am the true vine. My Father is the gardener."
>
> JOHN 15:1

The third spring, before the growing season began again, the gardener pruned back the spindly branches that had grown out of each arm. He snipped back the four long grape arms so that only two buds remained on each one—just right for bearing rich clusters of grapes.

From then on the gardener carefully pruned the branches every spring. The wise gardener knew that untrained and unpruned vines become a snarled mess, like tangles of hair. A pinch here and a cut there shape the vines and keep them growing in the right direction. Sunlight reaches more leaves. The vine is healthy and protected from disease. Plenty of energy is on hand to produce leaves and flowers and fat clusters of grapes.

God the Father is a gardener. Jesus is the vine. We're His branches.

Just as the earthly gardener prunes the branches of His vines, the heavenly gardener prunes us. He cuts out dead wood—parts of our lives that don't bear fruit for

Bananas grow on plants that are as big as trees. After the plant bears a bunch of bananas, the large "stem" is whacked back to the ground. This new stem grows to replace the first one and will produce more fruit.

CHECK IT OUT!

Take a nature walk in your backyard or nearby park. Pick out one tree. Does it need to be pruned? Here are some clues:

* Does it have crossed branches? Do some of them rub against each other?

* Are branches over-crowded?

* Do some branches look skinny and weak?

* Are some branches brittle? Do they snap easily? These branches are dead.

* Are some branches shriveled? These are sick.

DIG DEEPER!

* grapes
* pruning
* gardening

His glory. He cuts out extra leaves and branches to send energy into the branches that will bear fruit. He even "cuts away" some parts of our lives that bore fruit before.

How does He do all this?

He puts us in situations where we have to trust Him and believe what He's taught us. As we learn to take Him at His word and depend on Him, we bear fruit for His glory. So we shouldn't be surprised when difficulties come into our lives. Often it's the work of the heavenly gardener, shaping and training us into who He wants us to be.

Sometimes we might think its our responsibility to change our lives, to become what we think God wants us to be. But wouldn't it be funny to see an earthly grapevine try to prune itself? Our job is to remain in Jesus, to "hang out" with Him. As we trust Him, He does the rest. The heavenly gardener knows what He's doing. As He shapes, trains, and prunes us, our lives bring Him praise and glory.

Thought to remember:

God prunes me so I can bear more fruit for Him.

Additional verses:

John 15:5; Philippians 1:6; 1 Peter 4:12; Romans 5:3–5; John 6:28–29; Galatians 5:22–23 (NIV)

Have you ever visited an Internet Web site?

If so, then you probably know that one Web site is linked to another, and that Web site is linked to another, and so on . . . in a network called the Worldwide Web.

In the plant and animal world, there's a similar web. It's a connection of plants that are eaten by animals, and animals that are eaten by other animals, and so on . . . in a network called the food web. The food web is made up of food chains.

All living things need energy to live, grow, and make repairs to their bodies. Energy comes from food. Plants catch sunlight with their leaves and turn it into food. So the first link in any food chain is a plant, also called a **producer**. Because plants are the first link in any food chain, you could say that all food is a bite of sunshine! Some of this energy is stored in roots, stems, leaves, flowers, and fruit.

PRODUCER: (PRO-DUE-sir) something that makes its own food

Plants are linked to . . .

. . . any animal that eats plants. An example is a rat. It's called a **consumer**.

Rats are linked to . . .

. . . any animal that eats rats. An example is a cat. It's called a second-level consumer. Cats are linked to . . .

CONSUMER: (cun-SUE-mer) these eat PRODUCERs or other consumers, or both

. . . any animal that eats cats. An example is an owl. It's called a third-level consumer. Owls are linked to . . .

. . . any animal that eats them. Not many animals do that, so the chain usually stops like this—until the owl dies. Then **decomposers** such as bacteria take over. Decomposers break down plant and animal bodies for their own food. Some of this food is returned to the soil to be used again by plants . . . and rats and cats and owls.

In real life, a simple food chain expands into a food web because most creatures eat many kinds of plants and animals. Each is part of several food chains. Rats eat meat as well as several kinds of grasses, seeds, and berries. Cats eat lizards, insects, and birds. Owls eat mice, rabbits, and foxes. Insects eat plants and other insects. Lizards eat insects. Foxes eat rabbits and mice.

DECOMPOSER: (Dee-come-PO-zer)

Humans are also part of the food web. Are we producers or consumers? Since we're not plants—we definitely can't make food from sunlight—we're not producers. But all of

> [Jesus said,] "Love each other, just as I have loved you."
>
> JOHN 15:12

Do you enjoy eating mushrooms in salads, pizzas, or spaghetti sauce? You might be surprised to find out that when you eat mushrooms, you're eating a decomposer. Mushrooms are a type of fungus.

MATCH IT!

Below is a list of plants and animals. Pick a different color for each animal. Using the assigned colors, draw a web of lines to connect animals to the plants and animals they eat. For example, if you pick red for coyote, draw red lines from the coyote to all the plants and animals coyotes eat.

rat	tree leaves	coyote
rabbit	fruit	cat
mouse	nuts	fox
insect	shrub leaves	owl
cow	berries	raccoon
chicken	grasses	you
lizard	seeds	bear

The answers are on page 153.

us eat some sort of fruits, vegetables, and grains, so we're first-level consumers. Those of us who eat beef—which eat plants—are second-level consumers. And if we eat fish that eat other fish, that makes us third-level consumers.

When you think about all the different relationships between plants and animals on land and in water, you can see how the connections get pretty tangled. Each plant and animal, no matter how big or small, affects others in the web. The food web is a web of life.

We are also part of a different web of life.

Over three hundred years ago, a poet named John **Donne** wrote that "No man is an island." As you might guess, this means that every person is linked to other people in some way. If you wrote down each contact you had with people on a normal day, you might be surprised at how many there were. Every one of us is part of a network of many people.

Just as plant and animal lives affect each other in the food web, each day we also affect the lives of all others we're in contact with. Whether it's a friend, family member, store clerk, or even an enemy, our attitudes and actions toward others make a difference. Are we kind, helpful, and encouraging? Or are we grumpy, bad-tempered, and selfish?

God is interested in how our lives affect others. He lives inside us and wants to touch others through us. Because He is love, He wants to touch others with His love. Just as sunshine is turned to leaves, stems, and fruit in plants, God's sunshine is turned to love, joy, and peace in our lives—and those whose lives we touch.

DONNE:
(SOUNDS LIKE DONE)

Thought to remember:

My life touches and affects other people.

Additional verses:

1 John 4:7–9, 16; 1 Corinthians 3:9; 13:13;
2 Corinthians 3:3; 4:7; John 15:11

EXPLORE IT!

All you need for this activity is a lump of modeling clay and a roomful of people. Roll the clay into a ball. When you're gathered with a group of friends or family, pass around the ball of clay. Each person can hold the clay for as long as they want. When the clay returns to the first person who handled it, take a good look at it. Is it still shaped the same as when it started? As you can tell, each person who touched the clay had an effect on it. In a similar way, each person we're in contact with is affected by us. They also affect us.

DIG DEEPER!

* food chains
* food webs
* ecology

46 The Strange Strangler

strangler:
(STRANG-ler)

To discover
more about
Life in the rain
forest, turn
to "A Special
Place" on
Page 83.

T here's a killer in the jungle. It's not a leopard, a harpy eagle, or an emerald tree boa. It's a tree—a tree called the **strangler** fig. In the crowded world of the rain forest, plants grow at different levels depending on their differing needs for sunlight, soil, and water. Many plants need a lot of light but sprout in the shadows of the forest floor. It's a long way from the forest floor to the sunny upper levels of the canopy. After setting down roots, plants that love light must grow quickly in a race to reach the sun.

Strangler figs have a bizarre way to satisfy their need for sunshine. They've got it backward. They start out at the top of the world, not the bottom.

When a bird or bat eats a fig, it scatters tiny fig seeds in its droppings. Some seeds land in the gloom of the forest floor and sprout. But a few come to rest on the branches of trees. Here, the fig tree gets a head start cradled in the arms of another tree.

Drawing food from the moist air, the strangler fig sprouts and then grows roots that journey toward the ground. Some of these roots wrap around the trunk of the host tree.

Eventually the roots reach the ground. Now that the fig is able to soak up water and **nutrients** from the soil, growth takes on hyperspeed. High above, waxy leaves stretch out. Thick roots close their grip around the host tree. The host can no longer grow outward and its flow of water and nutrients is choked off. Slowly it is strangled and dies.

> When Peter saw [John,] he asked, "Lord, what will happen to him?" Jesus answered, "Suppose I want him to remain alive until I return. What does that matter to you? You must follow me."
>
> JOHN 21:21-22

nutrient:
(NEW-tree-ent)
ingredients
that feed
something
that's alive

Then the host tree rots inside the framework of strangler fig roots. Using the rotting host tree for additional food, the strangler fig continues to grow. Within a few years, the fig tree is a hollow network of gnarled roots. What began as a seed the size of a pinhead becomes a giant of the forest.

Do you have a strangler fig in your life? Of course you don't have a plant growing in the crook of your arm! But perhaps you have a strangler fig in your *spiritual* life. Many of us do.

A spiritual strangler fig grows when our attention is focused on other people instead of God. It begins when we play the "if only" game and think thoughts like these:

"If only I were as beautiful as Kristin."

"If only I were more athletic like Jerod."

"If only I could sing like Mark."

When we have our eyes on others, a small seed of a thought can grow into a giant tree. We become dissatisfied with our own lives. Like the host tree of the strangler fig, our spiritual lives are choked. We stop growing. Our inner lives rot.

The disciple Peter had the same problem. After Jesus told him about his future, Peter asked what would happen to another disciple, John. Jesus' response? What happened in John's life was none of Peter's business.

So how do we get rid of strangler figs in our lives?

By following Jesus.

When our eyes are on someone else, God can't lead us where He wants to take us. But as we keep the eyes of our hearts on Jesus, we forget about wanting to be different from what we are. We become satisfied with who we are. If we follow Jesus a step at a time, all sorts of possibilities open up for our own lives.

Thought to remember:
Follow Jesus.

Additional verses:
John 21:18–22; 8:12; Psalm 139:13–14; Colossians 3:4a; Jeremiah 29:11

Strangler figs begin life as "air plants," or **epiphytes** (EH-pih-fights). Epiphytes are plants that grow on the branches and leaves of other plants without stealing food from them. Instead, they pull moisture and nutrients out of the air and rain.

TRY IT!

The tubes that carry nutrients throughout a tree are cut off when the strangler fig blocks their growth. You have tubes—blood vessels—that carry nutrients through your body, too.

Squeeze your pointer finger tightly with the fingers of your other hand. What happens? Your finger will turn purple and cold when its supply of blood is cut off. Squeezed in this way, your finger would eventually die. This is similar to how a strangler fig chokes life from its host.

DIG DEEPER!

★ rain forest
★ tropical rain forest
★ plants
★ epiphytes

Have you heard the phrase "busy as a bee"?

Where do you think it came from? See for yourself. Shrink down to bee size, grow two antennae, and sprout a pair of wings.

Before you enter the hive, smear on a bit of honeybee smell so you can sneak past the guards. Once inside, you see that the hive is buzzing with activity.

Nearly all the bees are females, called workers. They are daughters of the same queen. In the first two to three weeks of their short, six-week lives, workers have jobs inside the hive. At first they feed larvae and clean out **cells** of honeycomb where new bees develop.

Some females are construction workers. Pulling flakes of wax from their abdomens, they build and repair honeycomb. Others plug holes with a sticky bee glue collected from plants. Workers put caps, or lids, on cells filled with honey. They also cap cells of larvae that are ready to change into adults.

Another of their jobs is to prepare food. Pollen brought into the hive is packed into cells. Sweet flower **nectar** is turned into honey.

Certain bees serve the queen. Her job is to lay eggs—up to three thousand each day! There's only one queen in a hive, and this makes her very special. She's always surrounded by a group of workers who feed and lick her and clean up after her. The queen produces a smell that keeps other queens from being raised.

Other indoor activities include housecleaning: Workers remove dirt and dead bees from the hive. Then, as they grow older, some workers become guards who protect the hive from intruders.

As workers advance from job to job, their bodies change to allow them to carry out new tasks. When they're finished with the job of feeding larvae, they can no longer produce "brood feed." Then workers are able to produce wax to build cells.

cells: six-sided wax cups that make up a honeycomb

To discover more about flowers and pollen, turn to "Voice of a Flower" on page 13.

nectar: (NECK-ter)

> GOD HAS PLACED EACH PART IN THE BODY JUST AS HE WANTED IT TO BE. IF ALL THE PARTS WERE THE SAME, HOW COULD THERE BE A BODY? YOU ARE THE BODY OF CHRIST. EACH ONE OF YOU IS A PART OF IT.
>
> 1 CORINTHIANS 12:18–19, 27

In the last two to three weeks of honeybees' lives, wax production stops. Females graduate to fieldwork. Their job is to gather water, nectar, and pollen, which are turned into bee food. When a worker crawls inside flowers, pollen grains stick to hairs on her body. Brushing pollen into baskets on her hind legs, she lugs it back to the hive.

Nectar is the syrup inside a flower. Bees stick their long tongues inside flowers and suck nectar into special honey stomachs. When full, workers make a beeline back to the hive. House bees sip nectar from the gatherers and store it in cells.

By now you might be wondering what happened to the males. Fatter and bigger than workers, male bees—or **drones**—don't have stingers or pollen baskets. They must be fed by workers, and their only job is to mate with a queen. Only about one in one thousand drones has a chance to mate. In the fall, they are driven out of the hive and left to starve and die.

DRONES: (DRONZ)

Now that you've seen the jobs of bees, do you think one is more important than another?

A queen might seem more important because she's the only one who lays eggs. But what would happen to a hive if there were no workers? Or drones? Even in a hive of 80,000 bees, every bee is valuable. They all join together to make one strong, healthy hive where they work and rest.

In a way, a colony of bees is like your body. Every part of you, from your tongue to your little toe, works together to help you live in this world. Some parts of your body can be seen, some can't. For example, no one ever sees your heart, but could you live without it?

If you belong to Jesus, you are part of *His* body. Jesus' body—or the Church—is made up of all the people who follow Him. Everyone in Jesus' body is given a gift to serve one another. As in a hive swarming with bees, every person in Jesus' body is special.

Some people might act like queen bees because the gifts they use are in the spotlight; they get more attention. But every follower of Jesus is just as important as every other follower. Whether we like to give to others, pray, or

When a hive gets too crowded, the queen leaves with at least half of the workers. These bees cluster together tightly on branches or buildings while scouts search for a new home. When bees swarm they're less likely to sting you. Beekeepers capture swarms by gathering them into containers.

Try your hand at honeybee trivia:

How many flights does it take for honeybees to collect enough nectar to make one pound of honey? *25,000.*

How many flowers do honeybees visit to supply you with one pound of honey? *2,000,000.*

About how many bees does it take to make one teaspoon of honey? *12.*

How many miles does a hive of bees travel to make one pound of honey? Over *55,000.*

DIG DEEPER!
* bees
* honeybees
* honey

DRAW IT!

Experiment on paper. Try to draw a human body made up of only feet or ears or hands. Now draw a face without a mouth or eyes. How well could these bodies function without the necessary parts?

MAKE IT!

Cut ten strips of paper. Write the name of a honeybee job on each strip (see list at end of this activity). Staple the ends of one strip together to form a ring. Loop the next strip through the first ring and staple its ends together. Do the same with the remaining strips. When you're finished, you will have a chain of honeybee jobs. If you take out one of the rings, what happens to the chain?

Queen: lay eggs

Worker: clean hive

Worker: feed larvae

Worker: fix and build honeycomb and hive

Worker: cap larva cells

Worker: store pollen and nectar; make bee food

Worker: take care of queen

Worker: guard hive

Worker: gather pollen and nectar

Drone: mate with queen

simply help out, we all work together to make the church healthy and strong.

You have a special part, too. No matter how big or little your position in His body of believers might seem, you are vitally important. Jesus doesn't want you to compare yourself with other people. He doesn't want you to wish you were somebody else. He wants you to be satisfied with who He made you. He made you perfect for the role you play in His body. Bee assured! You are important.

Thought to remember:

I am important.

Additional verses:

1 Corinthians 3:8–9; Romans 12:4–6

48 Positive Partnerships

In the sea lives an eel that is mean,
Who likes for his mouth to be clean—
So with a quick swish
He visits a fish
That thinks of his dirt as cuisine.

Would you stick your hand into the mouth of an eel or shark to clean its teeth? No way! But a finger-sized striped fish does more than that. It regularly swims inside the mouths of eels, sharks, and other fish that could eat it. Sea creatures regularly visit cleaner fish to have their teeth and gills cleaned, in the same way we visit the dentist.

Symbiosis:
(Sim-be-OH-sis)

Symbiosis is the name given to close relationships formed by many different species of animals.

In some cases of symbiosis, one partner is helped and the other is neither helped nor harmed. We call this **commensalism**.

commensalism:
(Kuh-MEN-Sul-iz-um)

You probably don't know it, but you're very close to some minimites that live on your face. These mites make themselves at home just under the skin at the base of your eyebrow and forehead hairs. Here they find a never-ending supply of skin cells to keep them happy for life.

> Two people are better than one. They can help each other in everything they do.
>
> ECCLESIASTES 4:9

If learning that you've got creepy-crawlies on your face makes *you* feel creepy, don't let it bug you. These itty-bitty beasts won't bother or harm you . . . they usually don't even itch.

Symbiosis is not always a one-way street, though. Togetherness that helps *both* partners is called **mutualism**.

mutualism:
(MEW-chew-ul-iz-um)

You can probably guess how the cleaner fish and its customers benefit from their strange friendship. Food is the cleaner fish's payment for picking off parasites, dead skin, and bits of food. This custom clean-up job keeps eels, sharks, and other fish healthy. When cleaner fish are removed from an area, many fish leave. Those that stay behind come down with skin diseases.

Another underwater companionship takes place between one species of hermit

Plants and animals form special friendships, too. One kind of tropical ant lives in acacia trees. These ants attack plant eaters that try to make a meal of the acacia. They also protect the tree from other plants that grow too close. In exchange, the tree provides hollow thorns for ant nests and special leaf tips for food.

crab and sea **anemones**.

Anemones have **tentacles** with tiny stinging threads that fire when touched. Yet hermit crabs wear sea anemones on top of their shells. Why? The anemone protects the hermit crab from octopus and other fish that would eat it. In exchange, the anemone feeds on the crab's leftovers and is carried to new feeding grounds. Even when the crab outgrows its shell and moves to a larger one, it brings the anemone along.

Other animals depend on odd friendships for survival, too. Termites eat wood, which they can't digest. Inside their stomachs are microscopic critters that digest wood for them. Without stomach partners, termites would starve. In exchange, they provide the tiny creatures in their stomachs with food and lodging.

Cleaner fish and eels, hermit crabs and sea anemones, termites and microscopic stomach partners are all creatures that are helped by special friends. These animals need each other. Their partners do something for them that they can't do for themselves.

The sea anemone is also involved in a close friendship with another sea creature, the clown fish. This bright orange fish is able to hang out in the dangerous tentacles of the anemone without harm. It's believed that the clown fish has special skin that keeps the anemone's tentacles from firing. In exchange for a safe place to live, the fish keeps the anemone free of dirt. It may also lure other fish near for the anemone to eat.

In our lives, we also have special relationships with others. God made each of us with different strengths and weaknesses. Because none of us is good at everything, we're like termites who can't digest food and fish who can't clean themselves. We need special friends to help out.

There are times in all our lives when we struggle or fall down. That's when we need another to give us a hand of encouragement.

There are hard times in all our lives when we feel like we can't even pray. That's when we need others to pray for us.

anemone:
(uh-NEM-uh-nee)

tentacle:
(TEN-tuh-cul)

Different species of African hoofed animals, such as zebras and wildebeests, sometimes gather in mixed herds to help each other out. Each brings its strengths in sight, hearing, or smell to increase their chances of picking up on predators.

There are times in all our lives when we're confused or need advice. That's when we need others to come alongside and point us toward God. We learn from each other.

As with mutualism, being partners is a two-way street. Not only do we need help, but we do the same for others.

Who are our symbiotic friends? They can be friends from our school or neighborhood. Our parents, grandparents, brothers and sisters, aunts and uncles, and teachers also fill these roles. Special friends are people we can trust and be honest with, and who can trust and be honest with us in return.

Do you have a special friend to encourage? To pray for? To share your life with? If not, ask God for one today.

Thought to remember:
I need others and they need me.

Additional verses:
Ecclesiastes 4:10–12; Proverbs 27:17; 1 Thessalonians 5:14 (NIV)

TRY IT!

Ask your parents or teachers to locate a "ropes" or "tree tops" course in your area. Then take your friends and family through it. These courses are designed so you have to climb through the tops of trees or telephone poles, but you can't do it by yourself. You will experience firsthand that you need one another to help you complete the course.

DIG DEEPER!

* symbiosis
* animal friendships
* commensalism
* mutualism

49 AN UNINVITED GUEST

NOURISHMENT: (NOOR-ish-ment) the things in food needed for life and growth

ectoparasite: (EK-toe-pair-uh-site)

To discover more about creatures that steal blood, turn to "Life-giving Blood" on page 24.

endoparasite: (EN-doe-pair-uh-site)

fluke: (flewk)

Suppose you and your family are at the dinner table. You're just about to enjoy a forkful of spaghetti when the front door opens. In walks a stranger. He pulls up a chair next to you and helps himself to your food. He's an uninvited guest to your table.

All over the world, uninvited guests take advantage of other living things to supply them with food. They're creepy, sneaky, ugly, and disgusting. Most are unseen.

What are they?

Parasites.

The word *parasite* actually comes from an old Greek word that means "the person who sat down to dinner uninvited." These are creatures who get close to plants or animals so they can rob **nourishment** from their bodies. The plant or animal it steals from—the host—is often hurt in the process. Parasites live in everything from worms, fish, and insects to plants, birds, and mammals.

Some parasites live on the *outside* of their hosts—these are **ectoparasites**.

Fleas, ticks, lice, and leeches are examples. When you're not looking, they sneak a sip of your blood.

Other parasites live *inside* the body, often for years. These are **endoparasites**.

Worms such as tapeworms, roundworms, hookworms, and **flukes** find homes in all sorts of animals.

Tapeworms are long and flat. Fish, beef, and pork tapeworms all live as adults in humans but spend part of their lives in fish, cows, and pigs. Humans become homes to these worms when they eat infected meat that hasn't been cooked thoroughly.

Flukes are tiny flatworms shaped like willow leaves. They also need different hosts as they develop from egg to adult.

One type of fluke lives its adult life in certain small birds in Europe. First, adult flukes lay eggs inside birds. The eggs are passed to the outside world in bird droppings. A hungry snail, poking along and eating grass, gobbles them up by mistake. Once inside the snail, the eggs hatch into larvae. Moving to the snail's liver, these lar-

> ANYONE WHO WALKS WITH WISE PEOPLE GROWS WISE. BUT A COMPANION OF FOOLISH PEOPLE SUFFERS HARM.
>
> PROVERBS 13:20

vae reproduce and change into another form. Now they must return to a bird host. How?

They travel—but not outside the snail. They travel to the snail's feelers, or eyestalks. The snail's slender eyestalks thicken and bulge as the parasites invade. Yellow, orange, and brown bands brighten them. They throb. Now the eyestalks look more like caterpillars than part of a snail. Tricked by the parasite, birds eat the young flukes along with the snail's feelers. Now the cycle begins again. Sounds like something out of a science fiction movie, doesn't it?!

Parasites are definitely something to avoid. Though they don't usually kill their hosts, they do sap the lives of those they infect. Parasites rob living beings of health and energy. They cause pain.

No one wants parasites in or on them. But sometimes we pick friends who are like parasites. These "friends" influence us to behave in ways that rob us of our emotional and spiritual health and energy. They cause us pain.

When someone is our friend, we may spend a lot of time with them. We do a lot of the same things—together. Because we're close, we influence each other. Before long, we act like one another. Can you see how a person can be close but harmful?

What are some signs that you're infected with a parasite?

- Perhaps your companion pressures you to disobey your parents or teachers.

- Perhaps she cheats and doesn't bother to do her homework. Before long, you think cheating might be okay, too. You've adopted a "why bother" attitude yourself, and now your grades are slipping.

- Or perhaps your buddy says unkind things about another good friend. Now you find that you're talking about that friend behind his back, too. And when you see him, you give him the frost treatment.

Take a look at your friends. Do you want to be like them? Do they encourage you to live a life you're proud of? Or does their influence drag you down?

If you're struggling with friends who are sapping your

Did you know . . .

- parasites have parasites? One-celled parasites live inside the fleas that live on dogs.

- if a parasite killed its host, its life would be in danger, too?

- each endoparasite can produce millions of eggs? Huge numbers of eggs increase the chances that one will hatch and make it to all the right hosts.

LIST IT!

Spend some time alone thinking about what makes a good friend. If you're unsure, ask a parent or other adult you trust. Write these qualities down. If you don't have a good friend, ask God to bring one into your life. If you do have a good friend, let God know how thankful you are. Let your friend know, too.

DIG DEEPER!

* parasites
* worms
* animal relationships

life, ask God to be your courage as you walk away. Ask Him for new friends—friends you can love and respect and who love and respect you!

Thought to remember:

I want to choose friends who don't drag me down.

Additional verses:

Proverbs 13:14; 22:24–25; Psalm 1:1 (NIV); 2 Corinthians 6:14b; Galatians 1:10

Are you part of the "in crowd" at school?

If not, would you like to be?

Who wouldn't? But whether we're part of the in crowd or not, it feels good to belong. As **social** creatures, most of us have a need to at least be included in a group.

Wolves are the same way. As social creatures, they belong to groups called packs. They depend on one another for safety, to hunt, and to raise their young. But sometimes wolves are cast out of their groups. How does this happen?

For a group of wolves to live together and carry out activities in an orderly way, each animal has a place. The relationships between wolves in a pack can be complicated, but the top wolves in a pack are the **alpha** male and female. Scientists believe alpha males are **dominant** over all other males in the pack, while alpha females are dominant over all other females. The next wolf in line is **submissive** to the alpha wolf above it, but dominant over others below it. And so it goes. Each member is submissive to the wolves ranked higher—but dominant over the wolves ranked lower—than itself.

The animal at the bottom of the pack, the **omega** wolf, is submissive to all others—not a fun place to be. It must often crouch, hold its tail low and ears flat, and lick the mouths of its bosses to acknowledge its low rank. When threatened by a dominant wolf, the animal at the bottom of the totem pole may roll onto its back, with its tail curled tightly to its belly.

Sometimes dominant wolves pick on the individual at the bottom of the pack. Several pack members may even band together to gang up on it. Driven to the edge of the group to avoid trouble, a submissive wolf may eventually follow at a safe distance. Still, pack members may chase and attack it. After a while the outcast falls one or two days behind the group.

Apart from their own kind, lone wolves have a hard time satisfying their hunger.

social: (SO-shul) likely to seek out the company of others. Social animals live with others of the same species rather than alone.

alpha: (AL-fuh) something that's first

dominant: (DAH-mih-nent) being in the top position and in control

submissive: (sub-MIH-siv) being under another's power or control

omega: (oh-MAY-guh) something that's last

> "The Lord himself will go ahead of you. He will be with you. He will never leave you. He'll never desert you. So don't be afraid. Don't lose hope."
>
> DEUTERONOMY 31:8

A wolf's position in the pack begins early in life. Through play fighting, pups learn one another's strengths and weaknesses. As adults, wolves are always on the lookout for a chance to raise their rank, though. Changes such as the loss or addition of a pack member can affect the social order.

Perhaps you're not an outcast, but enjoy the friendship of many friends or even belong to the "in crowd." If so, have you thought about leaving the comfort of your position to reach out to those who might be lonely or hurting? Here are some suggestions to get you started:

* Sit next to them if possible.

* Start a conversation. Begin with a greeting and a smile. Over several days work into a conversation about areas they may be interested in or things you may have in common.

* Be patient if progress seems slow. Remember that some people are shy and may take a while to trust others and open up.

* Be helpful or ask them if they can help you.

* Invite them to a get-together held at your house.

Some eat only after members of their former pack have had their fill and left. They may exist on small prey such as rabbits because it's hard to hunt deer, elk, or caribou on their own. For the lone wolf, survival is difficult.

As in the world of wolves, there are also human outcasts. Perhaps you know a kid who doesn't seem to belong with any group. He's just a little bit different—maybe his clothes aren't cool or he's not very outgoing. Maybe he's not very smart or maybe too smart. Other kids tease and pick on him. He just doesn't fit in and doesn't seem to have any friends. For the outcast, this world is a lonely place.

Perhaps that kid is you.

If so, here are some things to think about.

* Jesus was the greatest outcast of all time. He didn't fit in with top religious leaders of His day. Because Jesus didn't try to win any popularity contests, He was hated and rejected by the very men He had made. He understands how you feel (see Luke 6:7).

* Jesus promised that He would never leave or forsake you. It's a comfort to know that you're really not alone. This is a good chance to get to know God better (see Hebrews 13:5b).

* At some time or another, everyone in this world tries to get acceptance from other people. God wants us to get our acceptance from Him (see Galatians 1:10).

* God says that many of the first will be last and the last will be first (see Mark 10:31).

* Knowing that God accepts and cares for us frees us to be ourselves. It allows us to love our enemies and forgive them. **Bitterness** dissolves (see Romans 1:6; 8:31; Matthew 5:44).

* Some people have an easier time making friends and fitting in. But if that's not you, that's okay, too. While you're finding out where you belong in this world, God walks with you. Jesus promises to be your friend (see John 15:15).

ALL is not always lost for the omega wolf. It may eventually find a female to pair up with and start a family of its own.

bitter: (BIT-er) someone is bitter when they grow to hate or resent another

* Sometimes friendship problems don't lie with others, but with ourselves. Are you a cheerful, caring person? Do you smile at others and take a sincere interest in them? (see Proverbs 15:13a; 17:17).

Thought to remember:

I'm not alone. God is with me. He's my friend.

Additional verses:

Isaiah 53:3; Hebrews 4:15–16; Ephesians 1:4; John 15:16a; Romans 1:6; Galatians 1:10; Matthew 5:44

TRY IT!

Gather together five to seven people. Cut the same number of straws into different lengths. Draw straws. For ten minutes each person must obey anyone who has a longer straw than he has. Now give the longest straw to the person with the shortest one, and vice versa. Have the people in "the middle" switch around straws. Spend another ten minutes where each person must obey anyone who has a longer straw than he has. Discuss how each of you feels about your position.

DIG DEEPER!

* wolves
* social animals
* the social lives of animals
* solitary animals

Many animals can change colors.

Imagine.

If you were . . .

. . . a **ptarmigan**, you would change colors s-l-o-w-l-y with the seasons. Your summertime feathers are speckled—black, white, and brown. They help you blend in with rocks and dirt. As days grow shorter and colder, brown feathers fall out, white feathers sprout, and you fade into a snowy background. Then springtime warms the air and snow begins to melt. Patches of brown feathers grow in again. They match the surrounding patches of brown dirt and slushy snow.

If you were . . .

. . . a flounder, you would change colors to blend in with your environment, too. Other fish swim about freely, but you're a flatfish—your body looks like it's been squeezed through rollers. You spend your days lying with one side pressed against the ocean bottom, the other side—and both eyes—facing up. Sensors in your eyes and skin pick up the colors around you.

Not only can you change colors, but you can change patterns, as well. Against a sandy background, you turn a uniform sandy color. Against a pebbled background, you turn into—guess what? Splashes of colors give you that pebbled appearance. And if it's mud you rest against? No problem.

Camouflaged, you wait for shrimp and tiny fish to float by. It's as if the ocean bottom has a mouth. They never even see what eats them.

If you were . . .

. . . a crab spider, your colors would also hide you from prey. Skittering sideways—like a crab—you crawl to the center of a pink flower. Might as well make yourself comfortable. This is where you'll hang out for the next few hours, maybe days—as long as it takes for a fly or bee to buzz in for dinner. The last flower you visited was white, and so are you. But dinner will steer clear as long as you're a white spider on a pink flower. Time for a color change. Slowly your round body and long, skinny legs transform to a pretty pink. You melt into the background. Yesterday it was white,

Ptarmigan: (TAR-mih-gun) a large chickenlike bird that lives in the mountains and the Arctic

[Jesus said,] "I have called you friends."

JOHN 15:15b

The flounder is a master color changer. When tested against a checkerboard background, its skin turned a pattern of black and white splotches today it's pink, and tomorrow? Yellow might be nice.

Ptarmigans, flounder, and crab spiders change colors to fit in with their surroundings. Sometimes we act like color changers, too.

Around a particular group of friends, we act one way. Around a different group, we change our colors and act another. We don't want to stand out, to be *different*. Sometimes in order to fit into a group, we even cave in to peer pressure and do things we really don't want to do. We behave in ways that down deep we're ashamed of.

Why?

Because more than anything else on this earth, we want to be loved and accepted. Sometimes we'll do almost anything if others will just include us. And before we know it, we're doing things that we don't feel good about or that hurt us.

Friends who expect us to change for them aren't really our friends. True friends accept us as we are. They're worth waiting for, even if it means having the patience of a crab spider.

As hard as it is, rejection by our so-called friends for being ourselves isn't bad for us. It can force us to reach out and get to know God, the One who knows us through and through—and still accepts us just the way we are. We can depend on the Lord to be there for us. Knowing that He's the best friend we could ever have gives us the confidence to go out and show our true colors.

Thought to remember:

With God as my friend, I don't have to be a color changer.

Additional verses:

John 12:42–43; Romans 8:31; Proverbs 13:20; 17:17; 22:24–25

Chameleons' (kuh-MEAL-yun) color changes communicate fear, anger, contentment, and excitement. But changing colors can also control this lizard's body temperature. To warm up, a chameleon darkens its color to absorb more heat from the sun. But to cool off, it lightens its color. Lighter colors don't absorb as much heat.

TRY IT!

Explore the fun world of colors! You will need three clear drinking glasses, three spoons, food coloring, and water.

Pour water into each glass. Now add

* seven drops of yellow to glass number one

* three drops of blue to glass number two

* three drops of red to glass number three

What color do you get when you add

* one drop of blue to glass number one?

* two drops of red to glass number two?

* several drops of yellow to glass number three? (Hint: Because yellow is such a light color, you may have to add more drops to change the color.)

* several spoonfuls of color from glass number one to glass number three?

DIG DEEPER!

* animals that change colors
* camouflaged animals
* flatfish
* chameleons

Have you ever played follow the leader?

As the leader, you could put your hands on your head and skip across the room, and your followers trailed behind. But when you were a follower, you didn't think about what to do or where to go next. Your job was simply to follow the leader.

In the animal world there are followers and leaders. But to animals, following the leader isn't a game. Having leaders and followers brings order to a group of animals. Can you imagine what would happen if all animals in a group tried to lead? Order helps animals work together for protection, to find food and water, to raise young.

That's how it works in the world of wolves. A wolf pack is really a family, usually made up of a male, a female, and their young. Since wolf offspring stick around until they're two to four years old—when they're ready to start families of their own—the pack grows. Until they leave, older brothers and sisters help hunt. They protect and care for younger brothers and sisters.

To discover more about the social lives of wolves, turn to "Outcast" on page 121.

To keep order with all these family members, each has a position. The top dogs are usually the male and female that started the family. They're called the alpha male and alpha female. Below them are their oldest children. And below *them* are yearlings and pups.

Who chooses when to hunt, which moose or deer to chase, or when to call it quits? The alpha male and female. Who leads the way while the rest of the pack travels behind, single file? The alpha male—with the alpha female close at his heels. Who plows through chest-deep snow to break a trail? The alpha male. And who guards the wolf family? The alpha male and female! They're first to attack strange wolves.

Like wolf packs, African elephant herds are also made up of family members. A female lives her whole life with her mother, grandmother, daughters, sisters, cousins, and aunts. But a male leaves his family group when he's nearly a teenager. Then he

> WHEN HE HAS BROUGHT ALL OF HIS OWN SHEEP OUT, HE GOES ON AHEAD OF THEM. HIS SHEEP FOLLOW HIM BECAUSE THEY KNOW HIS VOICE.
>
> JOHN 10:4

lives alone or in loose groups with other bull elephants.

In an elephant herd, it's the oldest female in the family—called the **matriarch**—who's boss.

matriarch:
(MAY-tree-ark)

drought: (rhymes with sprout) a time when there isn't enough rainfall. Plants dry up and animals die.

Who knows where to find the best grazing areas? The matriarch. Who knows where to find water holes, especially in times of **drought**? The matriarch. Who charges with ears spread and trunk raised when animals or people threaten the herd? The matriarch. And who takes up the rear when the herd flees danger? The matriarch!

Like wolves and elephants, all who believe in Jesus are also part of a family—a family of sheep. And like wolves and elephants, we follow a leader. We follow Jesus, the Good Shepherd.

Who leads His sheep along the paths of life? The Good Shepherd. Who leads His sheep to rich pastures to feed their hearts? The Good Shepherd. Who leads His sheep to springs of living waters to satisfy their thirst—especially in times of drought? The Good Shepherd. Who searches for His sheep when they wander off to thorny places? The Good Shepherd. And who is even willing to give His life to protect His sheep from harm? The Good Shepherd!

As His sheep, our lives are simple. Our job is to follow our Shepherd. We aren't left alone to figure out what trails to take in life, to plow through deep snow, to find food and water, or to defend ourselves. We trust our leader to take care of all these needs for us.

It's a comfort to know that someone as important as God cares enough to lead us. What could be better than to hear the Good Shepherd say, "Follow me"? His command is simple enough for the weakest believer to obey.

Thought to remember:
Jesus leads me. He's my shepherd.
Additional verses:
Psalm 23; John 10:4–5, 11, 14–15; Isaiah 40:11; John 8:12; Proverbs 3:5–6

Female elk, called cows, also live in groups. As with elephants, the cow that leads the herd is an older animal. She knows the network of game trails that lead to pasture and safety. She's also familiar with migration routes traveled during spring and fall. If a lead cow is removed, the herd scatters in confusion.

EXPLORE IT!

What happens when everyone tries to lead?

Find a partner or two. While standing, place your palms together. Without speaking and without losing contact with your partners' palms, try to lead them where you want them to go. They will also try to do the same. Can you see what happens when everyone wants to lead?

DIG DEEPER!

✦ wolves
✦ elephants
✦ social lives of animals

53 Weakness Equals Strength

At first the scene is one of beauty. A blue-sky day, a pack of wolves traveling through a snow-covered meadow . . . The lead wolf stops suddenly and raises his nose to the air. The other pack members follow his cue—eyes, ears, and noses alert. Excited, they gather nose to nose, tails wagging. Silently, they turn onto a new course, tracking the scent of a deer.

In our minds, what happens next isn't so beautiful. The wolves continue toward the deer. As much distance as possible must be closed before the victim becomes aware of its attackers. Nearing their prey, they slow.

Surprised by its hunters, the deer freezes. So does each wolf. One minute, two minutes pass. The deer knows it's not powerful enough to fight off wolves. In an instant, it explodes from this standoff. The race for its life is on.

The outcome of this attack depends on several things. Did the deer get a big enough head start? How old is it? What kind of shape is it in? In the harsh world of nature, there's no room for weakness.

For prey species, weakness comes in several forms. . . .

> But He said to me, "My grace is sufficient for you, for my power is made perfect in weakness."
>
> 2 CORINTHIANS 12:9 (NIV)

A young, inexperienced animal may get separated from the protection of its mother. An old animal, no longer as quick as it once was, may not be able to outrun hungry hunters. The same is true for sick, wounded, or starving individuals. Healthy deer, moose, caribou, or mountain sheep are normally hard for wolves to bring down. A frail animal is overcome more easily.

What's the flip side of weakness? Strength. To survive, those that are hunted need muscle and might. So do those seeking mates.

RAM: a male bighorn sheep

Picture two bighorn sheep **rams** in a duel, charging each other. When they crash head-to-head, the thunder of their curled horns echoes through the canyons. Which animal wins? Usually the one with the more powerful body and largest horns. The prize? The chance to breed with more females.

Bull moose carry the largest antlers of any animal. As two males approach each other, they wave their weapons back and forth. This allows each animal to size up his

Male antler flies have small growths like antlers that rise from their cheeks. Two competing males press their antlers together and push. They push so hard that each fly rises to its hind legs, until the weaker bug falls backward.

competition *before* the battle begins. Any battle between animals with horns or antlers carries the risk of injury. A smaller or younger moose may prefer to retreat.

Males of many species compete in similar contests over females. Elephants smash heads, giraffes bang necks, and elephant seals slash each other with special daggerlike teeth.

In the world of nature, strength allows prey to escape from predators. It determines which males win the right to mate. Weakness brings death or defeat.

In our world, we also value strength. Of course we don't need strength to escape predators—or to win the attention of a girl or guy! But we admire strength in other forms: smart students who are tops in their class; runners, wrestlers, and soccer players who come in first; those who are the richest, the most beautiful, the most powerful.

The strange thing about human strength is that we value it, but God doesn't. What He values is weakness. Why? Because a weak person has to depend on God. Then when God uses that person, it's obvious who did the work!

Gideon:
(GID-ee-un)

Midianite:
(MID-ee-an-ite)

Take the story of **Gideon** in the Old Testament. During his life, the **Midianites** ruled over Israel. One day, the Lord told Gideon that He would send him to defeat the Midianites. Gideon was shocked—he was from the weakest group in his tribe. Worse, he was the least in his own family. The Lord assured Gideon that because He was with him, the Midianites would be overthrown.

When Gideon reported for battle, the Lord told him he had too many men. More than half returned home, but still there were too many. In the end, only three hundred men with trumpets and jars attacked armies so great they could not be counted.

But the Lord won through Gideon.

And He will through you, too. We can do nothing without Jesus. But we can do all things through Him because the weakness of God is far stronger than the strength of man.

When tasks or difficulties before you seem impossible, take courage. Rest in the Lord. Depend on Him to do His

Thomson's gazelles leap high into the air on straight legs when chased by African wild dogs. The gazelle that jumps the highest and most often is most likely to escape its hunters. Wild dogs seem to concentrate on gazelles with the weakest jumps.

CHECK IT OUT!

Read the story of Gideon in Judges 6:11–7:22.

When you're done, answer these questions:

1) How would this story have changed if Gideon had been strong?

2) How are you like Gideon?

3) What are areas of weakness in your life that God can use to reveal His strength?

DIG DEEPER!

✦ animal behavior
✦ how animals fight

The male mud-puddle frog of Central America uses songs to compete for mates. When alone he'll sing a quiet, gentle song to attract females. But if he's in the company of other males, he'll add a second lower-pitched stanza. The largest male wth the deepest voice wins. This second call is used less often because it also attracts hungry bats!

best through you. Remember—He's your strength. Nothing is impossible for Him.

Thought to remember:

God's strength is shown through my weaknesses.

Additional verses:

Philippians 4:13; 1 Corinthians 1:25; Colossians 1:29; 2 Corinthians 12:9–10 (NIV); 1 Samuel 17:47

54 Riddles of Life

Here's a riddle:

What travels by land but has no legs?
By air, but has no wings?
By sea, but has no fins?
Seeds.

They're everywhere, on the move, in many different ways. Seeds float, seeds fly, seeds tumble, seeds ride.

Why?

Because plants can't move. Their seeds have a better chance of growing into plants themselves if they travel away from the mother plant. Floating, flying, tumbling, and riding are a few ways seeds spread around the world to carpet the earth.

The wind plays a big part in **sowing** seeds. You've probably blown the puffed heads off of dandelions. The wind does the same, lifting the tiny white parachutes from the stalk of the plant up, up, up and far, far away. Milkweed and cattails are two other plants with parachute seeds that rise like clouds into the sky.

The wind carries grass seeds, too. They are tiny and light enough to ride the breath of the wind many miles from home. Plant helicopters also take to the air. Ripped from their branches by gusts of wind, maple tree seeds whirl through the sky to the ground.

Tumbleweeds don't leave the earth. The whole plant dries up and rolls along, blown by the wind, scattering seeds like pepper.

Seeds also ride on animals. Seeds with hooks grab on to an animal's fur when it brushes against the plant. Burrs and spear grass have probably hitched rides on you in the same way.

Instead of hooks, the common mistletoe has sticky seeds that cling to the beaks, feet, and feathers of birds. Seeds that land in the mud of rivers and ponds are carried

> Sowing:
> (SO-ing)
> Scattering or
> spreading
> seeds

> You have been born again by means of the living word of God. His word lasts forever. You were not born again from a seed that will die. You were born from a seed that can't die.
>
> 1 PETER 1:23

Violet seeds grow in a pod. The pod splits apart until it looks like three tiny boats. As these sections dry, they shrink and pop out seeds.

The fruit of the squirting cucumber has a stopper in one end. Pressure builds inside the fruit as it ripens, until the stopper is forced out. Seeds "squirt" out behind the stopper.

Sneezeweed seeds have tails that shrink and expand depending on the amount of moisture in the air. As the tails shrink and expand, the seed creeps forward.

FIND IT!

You are the scientist.

Hunt for five different types of seeds. Some places to look are your house, backyard, nearby park, field, or greenhouse. Compare the seeds for size, shape, covering, and weight. How does each seed scatter?

away on the feet of animals. Squirrels and jays forget about the acorns they bury. These nuts grow where they're "planted."

Some seeds make their journeys in the stomachs of animals and birds. Sometimes animals eat the fruit of a plant, and the seeds come out the other end in droppings.

Coconuts are too heavy to be carried by wind or animals, but they float. They drift across oceans to faraway islands, ready to grow.

Here's another riddle:

> What seed is invisible and is sown in the hearts of men?
>
> The exciting news that Jesus gives you an **abundant** life.

God wants everyone to hear it. But this kind of seed isn't carried by wind, water, or animals. This seed is carried by people like you.

Spreading seeds about Jesus happens when we talk to people. It happens through written words in letters and books and over the Internet. It happens through song and art. It happens when you're kind and when you help others. Wherever you are—at school, at home, in stores, on the sports field—even without saying a word, your life can be a living letter from God that touches people's hearts.

Sometimes you might compare yourself with others and wish that you were quieter, or that you talked more. You might wish that you were smarter, a faster runner, or a better artist or writer. God made you just the way He wants you to be. He's given you abilities that are perfect for the way He wants you to sow His seed to those around you.

Have you heard the Good News about Jesus and believed it? Do you want to pass it on? Like the seeds of plants, there are so many ways. One way isn't better than another.

To discover what invention was inspired by burrs, turn to "Nothing New Under the Sun" on page 144.

abundant: (uh-BUN-dent) full; more than enough

Thought to remember:

God made me a unique sower to spread the seed of His Good News.

Additional verses:

John 10:10b; Luke 8:11b; Romans 10:15, 17; Psalm 139:13; Isaiah 6:8; 2 Corinthians 3:3

EXPLORE IT!

Blow dandelion seeds into the wind. Follow one. How far does it travel?

DIG DEEPER!

* seeds
* how seeds travel

55 Fruit Facts

What's your favorite fruit?

Do you like peaches? Pears? Plums?

Perhaps you prefer more exotic fruits such as papaya, starfruit, or soursop.

Or do you go for the less juicy fruits—rice, squash, or walnuts?

Rice, squash, or walnuts? Are these really fruits?

Yes, they are. So are tomatoes, cucumbers, green peppers, pumpkins, and pecans.

Perhaps by now you're wondering what a fruit is, anyway.

To understand, it helps to look at how fruits develop. Let's start with a flower. . . .

Flowers are designed to help plants produce fruit with seeds inside. To do this, flowers have male and female parts.

Some plants carry both male and female parts on one flower. Some plants carry both male and female parts, but on *separate* flowers. But some plants are only male or female. Male plant parts grow on one plant, while female plant parts grow on a completely separate plant.

anther: (AN-ther)

pollen: (PAH-len)

The male part is a stalk with a club-shaped head, or **anther**, on top. Several stalks usually circle the center of the flower. The job of the anther is to form tiny grains called **pollen**.

Each type of plant makes its own special kind of pollen—some grains are round, some are star-shaped, some are oblong. They have outer coats that may be smooth, pitted, spiny, or wrinkled.

When pollen grains are ready, the anther splits open. Depending on the type of plant, these tiny particles are whisked away by wind, birds, insects, or water to the female part of the same type of plant.

stigma: (STIG-muh)

ovary: (OH-vuh-Ree)

While the anther is preparing pollen, the female part of a flower is getting ready to receive it. The female portion usually rises out of the center of the flower. Its long, graceful neck is topped by a sticky button, called a **stigma**.

At the base of the long neck is a rounded organ, called the **ovary**.

> YOU DID NOT CHOOSE ME, but I CHOSE you to go and bear fruit—fruit that will last.
>
> JOHN 15:16 (NIV)

Inside the ovary, egg cells form.

Now quiet action begins. Pollen is carried to the sticky female part, the stigma. The outer coat of the pollen opens. A tube grows down the long neck of the female part to the ovary. Then the pollen travels down this long tube to the ovary, where it joins with the egg cell and **fertilizes** it.

fertilize: (FUR-til-eyes)

While the fertilized egg cell develops into a seed, the petals and male parts of the flower wilt and fall off. The outer wall of the ovary swells into flesh, shells, or pods—what we call fruit. These protect precious seeds that will someday grow into new plants. By producing fruit, plants also provide us with food, refreshment, and life . . . a peach, pear, or plum . . . a green pepper, pumpkin, or pecan.

Bearing fruit is **vital** to the lives of many plants.

vital: (VIE-tul) very, very, very important

Bearing fruit is important to our lives, too. Jesus said that one of the purposes of our lives is to go and bear fruit. In this case, fruit isn't something we can sink our teeth into. It's the result of the Spirit of God's life in us: love, joy, peace, patience, kindness, goodness, faithfulness, gentleness, and self-control.

When we belong to Jesus, we want to please Him, and we want our lives to bring Him honor. God is honored when we bear fruit for Him. But if you've ever tried to be loving or patient all day, every day, you know that it's impossible. How can we bear fruit to God in our own human strength?

We can't. Trying to live like God in our own strength is impossible.

That's why we need Jesus. He said, "Apart from me you can do nothing" (John 15:5). So we trust Him to do the impossible in our lives. Day by day, moment by moment, we look to God to live His life through us. Jesus' life in us bears the fruit of His Spirit—joy, peace, patience, kindness, goodness, faithfulness, gentleness, and self-control. Then we'll even fulfill the one command that sums up all the others: to love each other in the same way He loved us.

Peaches, pears, and plums bring refreshment to those who eat them. As we walk in the Spirit and His fruit is produced in us, we, too, bring refreshment and life to those around us.

Did you know?

* The red flesh of a strawberry is an incredibly swollen base of the flower. The tiny tear-shaped parts that we call seeds are actually fruit. Each contains a seed.

* The fruit of a peanut is its dry outer shell.

* The fruit of the pea plant is its crisp pod.

* When you eat an apple, you're eating more than the fruit. The flesh we like to eat is formed from the base of the flower. The fruit is actually the core surrounding the seeds inside.

TRY IT!

Try to be loving, joyful, filled with peace, patient, kind, good, faithful, gentle, and self-controlled for a whole day. If you thought you could produce the fruit of the Spirit in your life when you started, you'll know you can't by the time the day is over. God never wanted us to try to live like Him in our own strength. He wants us to know that we need Him to produce fruit. This exercise will prove that we do!

Different types of fruits have different numbers of seeds:

* Plums, chrries, and almonds each carry one seed.

* Pea and bean pods each carry several seeds.

* Poppy capsules carry thousands of seeds.

* Some orchid capsules carry about half a million seeds.

DIG DEEPER!

* fruit
* plants
* seeds
* how seeds grow

Thought to remember:

I can depend on Jesus' life in me to bear fruit for God.

Additional verses:

John 15:5, 8; Galatians 5:22–23 (NIV); Galatians 5:16

They're everywhere—in our kitchens, our bathrooms,

our beds. They're in the air we breathe, the water we drink, the food we eat. They're in our hair, on our skin, and inside us.

Yet we can't hear them. And most of the time, we can't smell, taste, or see them, either.

What are they?

Microorganisms—forms of life so tiny we can see them only with the help of a microscope.

One type of microorganism is **bacteria**.

These tiny creatures are made of one cell. They come in three basic shapes: rod, round, and spiral.

Even though bacteria can't be seen with the naked eye, we can see their effects. Some are helpful to man. Species that eat the bodies of dead plants and animals keep the earth clean. They help make rich soil. Good bacteria live in our intestines to help digest food. Do you like cheese? Without bacteria we wouldn't have cheese *or* yogurt.

The bacteria we hear about most often are those that cause bad effects in our bodies. Perhaps you've known someone with **pneumonia** or **Lyme** disease. **Leprosy**, a sickness mentioned in the Bible, is caused by a rod-shaped bacteria.

You've probably seen the bad effects of bacteria in your food, too. The brown, mushy spots on apples are a sign that bacteria are at work. Bacteria is one of the microorganisms that causes foods to spoil.

A rotten apple doesn't look very tasty, so you wouldn't eat it. Sometimes you can't tell if bacteria is present, though. Chicken, eggs, and milk products can carry a bacteria called **salmonella**.

If left out in warm air, these rod-shaped bacteria multiply. It's usually not until several hours after you've eaten spoiled food that you know it. Stomach pain, nausea, and diarrhea are some of the symptoms of this type of food-borne illness.

microorganism: (MY-crow-OR-guh-nih-zum)

bacteria: (back-TEER-ee-uh)

pneumonia: (new-MO-nyuh) a type of infection in the lungs

Lyme: (rhymes with lime) a disease that's spread by deer ticks

leprosy: (LEH-pruh-see) a disease that affects the skin, nerves, and muscles

salmonella: (sal-muh-NEL-uh)

> DO NOT WORK FOR FOOD THAT SPOILS. WORK FOR FOOD THAT LASTS FOREVER.
>
> JOHN 6:27a

Bacteria have a special way to survive conditions that could kill them. They grow tough cases around important parts they need for life. Protected in this way, bacteria can survive for years.

You've probably seen another microorganism that causes bread and fruit to spoil. It's called mold. This member of the fungi family looks fuzzy as it grows on oranges, bread, and other foods.

TRY IT!

Why do we keep apples in the refrigerator? Cooling foods slows down the growth of microorganisms that cause decay. Is this really true?

Take two apples. Place one in the refrigerator and one on your kitchen counter. Check the apples daily for signs of decay. Does the apple kept at room temperature spoil more quickly than the one left in the refrigerator?

Another type of food poisoning caused by bacteria is **botulism**.

Like the critters that cause leprosy and salmonella, these bacteria are also rod-shaped. But they live mostly in soil and grow only in places starved of air.

In countries where foods are canned carefully, botulism is rare because high temperatures kill the bacteria that produce the poison. But if canning of vegetables or meat isn't done carefully, the bacteria grow and multiply. They produce a poison that makes you sick. This poison can't be seen or smelled and is as deadly as cobra venom. A person who eats this spoiled food suffers nerve damage, becomes paralyzed, and often dies.

How do you avoid spoiled food?

* Many species grow best in warm air. Keep meats, eggs, and dairy foods in the refrigerator to slow down bacterial growth.

* Wash your hands before and after you handle food products. Wash the utensils used to prepare these foods.

* Cook eggs and meats completely to kill any bacteria.

Any food that isn't preserved will spoil. In fact, nothing from this world lasts forever.

While Jesus lived on earth as a man, thousands of people followed Him. Some came because they were hungry, so He fed them. But Jesus knew they had a much greater need than bread for their bodies.

That's why Jesus told them not to waste their lives working for food that spoils. He knows how easy it is for us to get caught up living for the temporary things of this earth. There's more to life than the things we see—things that turn mushy and decay.

Instead, God tells us to work for the food that lasts forever.

How do we do that?

By believing in Jesus. He's the Bread of Life. Jesus' life can't spoil because He's eternal. He lives on and on and on. Believing in Jesus gives us something here on earth that

botulism: (BOT-chew-liz-um)

can't spoil—His life in our spirits. Then our spirits live on and on and on.

Believing in the Bread of Life gives us life that can't spoil. Then while we live and work by faith on this earth, the needs of our hungry hearts are satisfied.

Thought to remember:

Jesus, the Bread of Life, gives me life that doesn't spoil.

Additional verses:

Matthew 6:19–21, 25, 33 (NIV); John 6:29; 1 Peter 1:3-4

DIG DEEPER!

* microorganisms
* bacteria
* fungi
* microbes

No school, swimming pools,
Sizzling sun, friends and fun,
Lazy days, lemonade—
Yahoo!
These are signs of summer.

So are butterflies. On warm summer days, they float from flower to flower on bright, stiff wings.

Butterfly wings don't start out straight and stiff, the way we recognize them, though. They have a strange beginning.

To discover more about how insects develop, turn to "The Marvels of Metamorphosis" on page 22

You may already know—a butterfly begins life as an egg. The egg hatches into a caterpillar, or larva. This caterpillar eats and grows and eats and grows until it becomes too fat for its skin. The skin splits and out crawls a larger caterpillar.

molt: (rhymes with bolt) an insect sheds its skin when it molts

A caterpillar **molts** several times like this. Finally, it stops eating. Hanging from a branch or leaf, the skin splits one last time. Underneath is not another caterpillar, but a **chrysalis**.

chrysalis: (KRIS-uh-lis)

Inside the chrysalis, the caterpillar transforms into a butterfly.

May the God of hope fill you with all joy and peace as you trust in Him, so that you may overflow with hope by the power of the Holy Spirit.

ROMANS 15:13 (NIV)

On a warm day, the chrysalis breaks open. What struggles free is a butterfly with a swollen body and damp, crumpled wings. The reborn butterfly hangs quietly with its wings closed. It pumps bloodlike fluid from its body into **veins** in its wings. Like a blooming flower, the tiny wings unfold. They increase in size. The butterfly's body slims down.

vein: (vane) a branching tube that carries body fluid—such as blood— throughout a body

Over several hours, the wings reach their full size. They dry and stiffen. After a few practice flaps, the butterfly takes off to visit a flower and sip its first meal.

But what happens if the butterfly falls from its perch before its wings expand and dry? Or if a wing vein is cut? Or if it's raised by a human who keeps it in a jar too small for it to spread its wings?

The wings dry in their wrinkled form. These aren't strong, graceful wings that carry the butterfly from flower to flower. They're useless limbs that cripple the butterfly. It can't fly. It can't eat. For the butterfly whose wings don't stretch fully before they harden, it's too late.

Are there situations in your life about which you feel "it's too late"?

Perhaps you're sorry about something you've said to family members or friends. As soon as the words came out of your mouth, you wished you could take them back. Perhaps you stole something from a friend and now you feel guilty. Perhaps you have a bad habit you just can't kick. You've messed up, and now you doubt you can be forgiven—especially by God. In your eyes you're the hopeless butterfly with crumpled wings.

But with God it's never too late. Whether your family or friends will forgive you or not, God always will. He's always waiting for you with open arms.

Or maybe it's someone else you're troubled about. Do you have a parent, brother or sister, or friend who has harmful habits? Maybe they need to come to the Lord. They're the injured butterfly with the wilted wings.

With God, it's never too late. We can't make someone else turn to God, but *we* can turn to God; we can pray. God is a God of miracles. He's able to work even in impossible situations. He can take crumpled wings and make them straight and strong, able to fly.

And even if the changes we prayed for don't come as we'd longed for, when we turn to God and put our trust in Him, we can fly on the sturdy wings of hope. His presence chases away hopelessness. Trusting in Him fills us with joy and peace.

It's never too late for us to turn to God.

Thought to remember:
There's always hope in God.

Additional verses:
Psalm 16:11 (NIV); 42:11; Romans 5:3–5; 15:13; Matthew 19:26; Luke 1:37; Jeremiah 32:17; 1 Corinthians 13:6–7; James 5:13

The dragonfly is another insect that starts out with shriveled wings. It sits quietly and pumps fluid into its silver wings before zipping off into the summer sky.

TRY IT!
For this activity you need two long balloons. Inflate one balloon and tie it off. Tie the second balloon around the middle of the first one. Blow air into the second balloon. What happens to the section of balloon that is starved of air? This is a picture of a wing that doesn't receive the fluid it needs to fully expand.

DIG DEEPER!
* butterflies
* dragonflies
* insects

58 Megamoth

If you saw one fly through the rain forests of Indonesia, you might mistake it for a bird. In fact, because of its oversized wings and fat body, you might mistake it for a *large* bird. But this graceful creature doesn't sail through skies on feathered wings, and it isn't a bat. It's an insect with scaled wings . . . a megamoth . . . the Atlas moth.

With a wingspan of nearly twelve inches, the Atlas is a giant among moths, topping the scale for size. But size isn't the only feature that makes this moth magnificent. Its reddish brown wings are decorated with a complex design of lines, scallops, and colors. A see-through triangle—thought to confuse predators—adds a finishing touch to each wing.

Add details about the Atlas moth's life to its size and beauty, and it becomes even more awesome. Atlas moths live only about a week, which means its **lifespan** is as narrow as its wings are wide. Most butterflies and moths have a feeding tube, or **proboscis**, with which they suck nectar from flowers. But the Atlas moth doesn't. Its life is so short, it doesn't need a proboscis. The Atlas lives completely on fat stored in its body while it was a caterpillar.

Since the female can't eat, her body is extra big so she has enough energy to produce the eggs she must leave behind. To save energy, she flies very little. Instead, the male Atlas moth is drawn to her by a chemical she puts out. He picks up the chemical with his feathery antennae, following the trail until he finds her. Once they mate, the female lays her eggs and dies. The male may seek out other females, but within a week to ten days, he dies, too.

It may seem strange that the life of a creature as grand as the Atlas moth is over so quickly. But it's not alone. The Atlas belongs to a whole family of moths without mouths. And many other adult insects also have short lives. Mayflies and fig wasps live only for a few hours or days. To a biologist, an animal's success doesn't depend on how long it lives. The purpose of an animal's life is to survive in its environment and leave behind as many offspring as possible.

Life-span: the average length a living thing can be expected to live

Proboscis: (PRO-BOSS-iss)

> For me, life finds all of its meaning in Christ.
>
> PHILIPPIANS 1:21a

If the purpose of an animal's life is to leave behind as many offspring as possible, what's the purpose of a human's life?

If you asked several people, you'd probably get a rainbow of answers. Some might say they want to make a lot of money, be famous, or have a good job and a nice house. Others might say a good marriage, having a happy family, or helping others are important goals in life. Perhaps others might say serving or loving God gives their lives the most meaning.

Like the Atlas moth, our lives pass by quickly. Of course, our life-span is much longer than a moth's! But compared with eternity, our lives last only a short time, like a morning mist that vanishes by noon.

Since our lives are so short, it makes sense that we would want to make the most out of them. What does God want for His children?

God wants His life to be revealed in us.

Before we believe in Jesus, we're separated from God. There's no way our lives can honor Him. But when we believe in Jesus, He comes to live inside us. As we walk with God, learning to depend on His life within us, His amazing life is revealed in and through us.

As God lives through us, His purposes are accomplished in our lives. That brings glory to Him.

Thought to remember:
I want Jesus' life to be shown through me.

Additional verses:
Psalm 39:4–5 (NIV); 103:15–17; Galatians 1:15–16a; Colossians 1:25b–27; 2 Corinthians 4:6–7; Matthew 5:16

The luna moth is another short-lived moth-without-a-mouth. In the same family as the Atlas moth, this large night flier has lime green wings, about four to five inches wide. Each hind wing has a tail up to three inches long. The luna moth lives in the eastern and southern areas of the United States.

LIST IT!
Make a list of friends and family—kids and adults. Ask each person this question: What do you think the purpose of your life is?

Write down each person's answer. Did you get a lot of different answers? Are answers from adults different from answers from kids? Why do you think it's valuable to have God's view on what's important in life?

DIG DEEPER!
* butterfly
* moth
* insects

59 Nothing New Under the Sun

We're surrounded by inventions that have changed our lives or made them easier. Velcro, barbed wire, paper, flashlights, pottery, and helicopters are just a few. Where did we get the ideas for these inventions? Many are borrowed from nature.

Velcro from nature? Can that be true?

Yes. The burr from a burdock plant has tiny hooks on the ends of each point. These hooks grab on to the fur of animals that brush against them. Hitchhiking is the burdock plant's way of spreading its seeds.

One side of Velcro looks like tangled hair, and the other is made of rows of hooks. The hooks are like the hooks of burdock burrs. They latch on to the tangled fibers on the other side.

Plants have also sparked ideas for other inventions. Barbed wire is one of them. What types of plants might encourage the development of wire with spikes? Plants with thorns and needles, such as roses and cactuses. The prickly parts of plants and the barbs on wire are meant to keep out trespassers.

Paper is another invention taken from nature. The nests of paper wasps are the inspiration. These wasps scrape up wood particles and mix them with **saliva**. From this material the wasp forms a paper nest.

saliva: (suh-LIE-vuh) also known as spit

The design for flashlights also came from an insect. Perhaps you live where fireflies sparkle on warm summer nights. The firefly's tail glows like a flashlight to attract mates.

We also may have copied the work of another insect—the potter wasp. As its name suggests, the potter wasp shapes mud pellets into pots for her eggs. Hand-built clay pots formed by humans are very similar.

Still *another* insect suggests the invention of the helicopter. Dragonflies zip through

> Everything that has ever been will come back again. Everything that has ever been done will be done again. Nothing is new on earth. There isn't anything about which someone can say, "Look! Here's something new." It was already here long ago. It was here before we were.
>
> ECCLESIASTES 1:9–10

the air or hover on whirling wings. Of course, helicopters don't have wings, they have blades. But the idea is the same. Like dragonflies, helicopters fly up, down, and sideways. They can also hang in one place.

Velcro, barbed wire, paper, flashlights, pottery, and helicopters are only a few of many amazing designs that man has copied from nature. Perhaps you can think of others. Where did they all come from? Did they happen by chance?

No! They came from God, who is the Creator of everything in the heavens and on the earth. That's why these designs are so amazing. They reflect the Maker. From astonishing dragonfly wings to simple dandelion parachutes, God's wisdom and creativity are illustrated. Bright colors of neon fish and butterfly wings show His beauty. The bothersome mosquito, with its needle-like mouthpart that draws blood, shows God's attention to detail.

These are only shadows of God, though. Because He's the Creator, He's more wonderful than anything created. His wisdom, greatness, and beauty can't be measured.

So when man borrows a form from nature to invent something to help society, he's really borrowing from God. These designs aren't new and improved, but imperfect copies of God's handiwork. He's the original Designer. Nothing new can be found under the sun.

insulation:
(iN-suh-LAY-shun)
a material used
to keep heat in
or out

hacksaw:
(HACK-saw)
a saw with fine
teeth, used to cut
through metal

Thought to remember:
God made all things. There is nothing new under the sun.

Additional verses:
Genesis 1:1; John 1:3; Psalm 104:24; Colossians 1:16–17; Revelation 4:11

The airplane is probably one of man's greatest inventions. But it took centuries for humans to figure out how to fly like birds. Even the jet is a copy of nature. Squids squeeze water out the back of their bodies; this pushes them forward. Jets move forward in a similar way.

MATCH IT!

Match the following words to discover more of man's inventions that are found in nature.

	saw grass
wax	porcupine quills
sponge	bee
radar	bird's beak
insulation	bat
air conditioning	mosquito mouthpart
snowshoes	living sponge
drinking straw	termite mound
hacksaw	
nutcracker	down feathers of ducks and geese
sewing needle	snowshoe hare

The answers are on page 153.

# DIG DEEPER!

* inventions of nature
* animal inventions

Do you like a good mystery? Most of us do.

It's fun to try to solve the crime before the answer is revealed at the end of a book. Scientists love a different kind of mystery. They try to unlock the secrets of nature. The life of the European **eel** is a mystery scientists have worked on for many years.

Baby eels hatch from eggs in the **Atlantic Ocean**, far off the eastern coast of the United States. Tiny and clear, at first they look nothing like their parents. But as these see-through eels make their way across the Atlantic, their bodies narrow. They sprout chest fins. By the time they reach the shores of Europe, young eels—or **elvers**—look like mini-eels.

Once they reach land, the females head inland to **fresh water**, swimming up rivers. Here they stay for the next eight or nine years, turning yellow and growing to about four feet in length. Scientists think that males linger along the coast in salt water for about three years. Compared to females, they're one-and-a-half-foot dwarfs.

Near the end of their stay in Europe, eels transform into silver adults with big eyes. Now it's time to mate. In the fall, swarms of female eels swim toward the sea. If necessary, they wriggle over soggy land to reach streams and rivers that empty into the ocean. Retracing the route across the Atlantic, these odd eels return to the place where they hatched. At last they lay eggs and die.

How do young eels find their way through deep ocean waters to the rivers of Europe and back again?

That's the mystery. The world is packed with similar puzzles.

Spider web weaving is one of them.

Nest building in birds is another. The tailorbird folds the edges of a leaf together and pokes holes in it with its beak. A few stitches with spider silk hold the leaf together in the shape of a nest. Female potter wasps build clay pots for their eggs. These pots are stocked with paralyzed caterpillars for baby wasps to eat when they hatch. How does a potter wasp build a pot the first time like every other female potter wasp?

---

eel: (rhymes with heel) don't be fooled—eels may look more like snakes, but they're fish

Atlantic Ocean: (At-LAN-tic) the ocean that separates North and South America from Europe and Africa

elver: (EL-ver)

fresh water: water that isn't salty

To discover more about how spiders weave webs, turn to "To Spin A Web" on page 71.

How very rich are God's wisdom and knowledge! "Who can ever know what is in the Lord's mind? Or who can ever give him advice?"

ROMANS 11:33a, 34

Scientists who study nature have a way to explain such mysteries. These are built-in behaviors. Every young European eel knows how to get to Europe because it's programmed to do so. This is called **instinct**.

Spiders weave webs, birds sew nests, and wasps build pots by instinct.

instinct:
(IN-stingkt)

Behind this answer is an even bigger mystery, though. How were all these creatures programmed with instincts to begin with?

This is a mystery that can't be explained without God. How God built instincts into the animals He created is something we may never understand. It's beyond our human power to explain.

There are many such mysteries surrounding God. How can He have no beginning or end? How can He be everywhere at one time? How can He know everything?

Perhaps one of the greatest mysteries of all is God's love. Can you imagine what kind of love God must have for us that He would come to earth in the form of a man? That He would allow himself to be nailed to a cross? That He would live inside us—those He created?

Trying to understand the mysteries of God can be like trying to find the end of a rainbow. But not being able to solve the mysteries of God isn't meant to trouble us or make us shrink away from Him. No, mysteries that can't be solved make us realize how great God is, and we're filled with wonder. Face-to-face with such an amazing God, our hearts can only answer by bowing down before Him in awe.

Thought to remember:
God is awesome!
Additional verses:
Isaiah 40:12–14; Job 37:23a (NIV); Revelation 4:11; Colossians 1:26–27; Ephesians 3:18–20; John 3:16

How does one species of goose rescue eggs that have fallen out of the nest? By instinct. The goose reaches for the stray egg with its long neck. With chin resting on the egg, the goose moves its head back and forth as it rolls the egg toward the nest. If the egg is removed by a scientist before it reaches the nest, the goose doesn't stop. It continues this "egg-rolling" behavior—all the way back to the nest!

TRY IT!
Here's a mystery. What is liquid and solid at the same time?

Flubber.

Make some and see for yourself. *Warning: Flubber is as messy as it is fun. It's best to play with flubber outside.*

Mix a half cup of cornstarch with one tablespoon of water.

Add more water, a little at a time, until you can form a hard ball with the cornstarch.

Flubber is hard when you squeeze it, but it melts when you hold it in your hand . . . or when you throw it.

DIG DEEPER!
* animal behavior
* animal instincts
* animal architecture

Acknowledgments

While working on *Glow-in-the-Dark Fish*, I was often amazed at the web of connections within the natural world. So it is in my own life. I am grateful to those who helped with this book.

A special thanks to Steve, Josh, and Daniel, who always listened—even if they did sometimes groan.

Mary Fritts, Mary Peace Finley, and Carol Reinsma faithfully provided valuable critiques. Pam Sheldon and Teri Dailey were always willing to encourage and pray.

Thanks to Rochelle Glöege, Senior Editor at Bethany House Publishers, for giving me this opportunity. And to Natasha Sperling, also of Bethany House Publishers, for her encouragement and suggestions.

Carol March and Ken Pals sifted through pages of reference materials to check science facts. George Brinkmann and John Watts of the Butterfly Pavilion and Insect Center in Westminster, Colorado, verified plant, butterfly, and moth facts. Darlene Kobobel, of the Wolf Rescue Center in Lake George, Colorado, patiently enlightened me on the details of wolf family life.

Thanks also to Jane Sanborn, who allowed me to use the recipe for "flubber" found in her book *Bag of Tricks II*; the National Honey Board for providing honey trivia; Barbara Bates of the Colorado State University Cooperative Extension, who reviewed the readings on plants; and Dave Michaux for giving on-the-spot, helpful advice.

Answers to Explore It! in chapter 1, "The Master Plan":

The next three Fibonacci numbers are 377, 610, and 987.

Answer to Find It! in chapter 3, "The Plague":

What is the cure for sin? Jesus!

Answers to Match It! in chapter 11, "All in the Family":

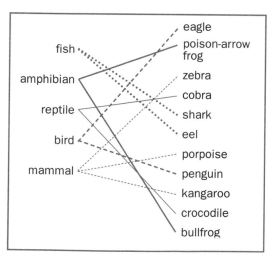

Answers to Find It! in chapter 12, "What's in a Name?":

A NAME NO ONE KNOWS BUT HIMSELF	FAITHFUL	ONE AND ONLY
	FATHER	
BEGINNING	GOD ABOVE ALL GODS	SAVIOR
COMFORTER		FIRST
CREATOR	JUDGE	LAST
END	LORD	TRUE
	MORNING STAR	WORD OF GOD

```
G O D A B O V E A L L G O D S
A N M O R N I N G S T A R D P
N E G S G B F A Q L Y C V S J
A A N I A F T A X X W O K U E
M N I D L V O S T Z U P D O L
E D N I A M I D L H R G G D U
N O N C O M F O R T E R K S F
O N I I D X R P R O U T B H
L G S L D K I W J W Y T U T
N Y E V R A C R O T A E R C I
E Z B N S U S S D M T P U A A
K N O W S B U T H I M S E L F
```

Answers to Name It! in chapter 14, "Who Needs Parents?":

chicken: chick

goat: kid

porcupine: porcupette

elk: calf

goose: gosling

fish: fry

eel: elver

sheep: lamb

seal: pup

zebra: foal

lion: cub

llama: cria

kangaroo: joey

skunk: kit

Answers to Match It! in chapter 20, "Amazing Armored Animals":

mouth guard: hockey, football, boxing

helmet: construction work, mountain biking, hockey, football, police work, baseball, inline skating, motorcycling

shin guard: hockey, soccer, inline skating

wrist guard: inline skating

chest pad: hockey, baseball

knee pads: football, inline skating

ear protection: construction work, wrestling

gloves: construction work, mountain biking, hockey, baseball, boxing, motorcycling

shoulder pads: football

bulletproof vest: police work

face mask: hockey, baseball, fencing

steel-toed boots: construction work

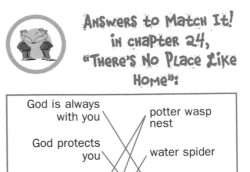

Answers to Match It! in chapter 24, "There's No Place Like Home":

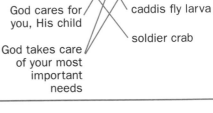

God is always with you

God protects you

God cares for you, His child

God takes care of your most important needs

potter wasp nest

water spider

caddis fly larva

soldier crab

Answers to Find It! in chapter 34, "A Special Place":

ANTEATER	GECKO	SLOTH
BEE	LEMUR	TAPIR
BOA	PANGOLIN	TERMITE
BUSH BABY	PARROT	TIGER
CHAMELEON	POISON-ARROW	TOUCAN
FROG	PYTHON	
FRUIT BAT	RED-EYED TREE FROG	

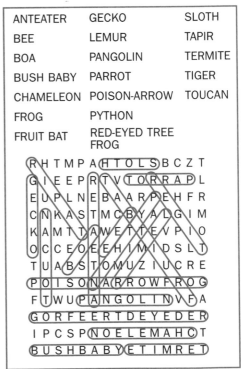

Answers to Match It!
in chapter 45,
"Take a Bite of Sunshine":

rat: nuts, berries, seeds, mice, other rats

rabbit: grasses

mouse: grasses, nuts, seeds, insects

insect: tree leaves, shrub leaves, grasses, seeds, other insects

cow: grasses, seeds

chicken: seeds, insects

lizard: insects

coyote: fruit, nuts, berries, rats, rabbits, mice, insects, chickens, lizards

cat: rats, mice, insects, lizards

fox: fruit, rats, mice, insects, chickens

owl: rats, rabbits, mice, cats

raccoon: nuts, berries, seeds, mice, insects

you: fruit, nuts, berries, grasses, seeds, rabbits, insects, cows, chickens

bear: leaves, fruit, nuts, berries, grasses, seeds,
    rabbits, mice, insects

Answers to Match It!
in chapter 59,
"Nothing New Under the Sun":

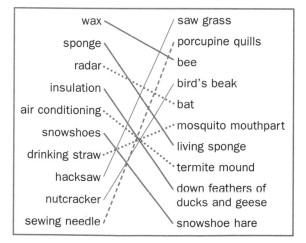

BETHANY BACKYARD®

PICTURE BOOKS

Spunky's First Christmas
   by Janette Oke
Spunky's Camping Adventure
   by Janette Oke
Spunky's Circus Adventure
   by Janette Oke
Annie Ashcraft Looks Into the Dark
   by Ruth Senter
Cows in the House
   by Beverly Lewis
Princess Bella and the Red Velvet Hat
   by T. Davis Bunn

Making Memories
   by Janette Oke
Hold the Boat!
   by Jeremiah Gamble
Annika's Secret Wish
   by Beverly Lewis
Fifteen Flamingos
   by Elspeth Campbell Murphy
Sanji's Seed
   by B. J. Reinhard

BOARD BOOKS
   by Christine Tangvald

God Made Colors...For Me!
God Made Shapes...For Me!
God's 123s...For Me!
God's ABCs...For Me!

REBUS PICTURE BOOKS
   by Christine Tangvald

The Bible Is...For Me!
Christmas Is...For Me!
Easter Is...For Me!
Jesus Is...For Me!

FIRST CHAPTER BOOKS
by Janette Oke

Spunky's Diary
The Prodigal Cat
The Impatient Turtle

This Little Pig
New Kid in Town
Ducktails

NONFICTION

Glow-in-the-Dark Fish and 59 More Ways to See God Through His Creation
   by B. J. Reinhard
The Wonderful Way Babies Are Made by Larry Christenson

Young Readers' books

SERIES FOR YOUNG READERS*
From Bethany House Publishers

THE ADVENTURES OF CALLIE ANN
by Shannon Mason Leppard
Readers will giggle their way through the true-to-life escapades of Callie Ann Davies and her many North Carolina friends.

ASTROKIDS
by Robert Elmer
Space scooters? Floating robots? Jupiter ice cream? Blast into the future for out-of-this-world, zero-gravity fun with the AstroKids on space station *CLEO-7*.

JANETTE OKE'S ANIMAL FRIENDS
by Janette Oke
Endearing creatures from the farm, forest, and zoo discover their place in God's world through various struggles, mishaps, and adventures.

BACKPACK MYSTERIES
by Mary Carpenter Reid
This excitement-filled mystery series follows the mishaps and adventures of Steff and Paulie Larson as they strive to help often-eccentric relatives crack their toughest cases.

THE CUL-DE-SAC KIDS
by Beverly Lewis
Each story in this lighthearted series features the hilarious antics and predicaments of nine endearing boys and girls who live on Blossom Hill Lane.

RUBY SLIPPERS SCHOOL
by Stacy Towle Morgan
Join the fun as home-schoolers Hope and Annie Brown visit fascinating countries and meet inspiring Christians from around the world!

THREE COUSINS DETECTIVE CLUB®
by Elspeth Campbell Murphy
Famous detective cousins Timothy, Titus, and Sarah-Jane learn compelling Scripture-based truths while finding—and solving—intriguing mysteries.

*(ages 7–10)

11/00